Batter's Castle

BATTER'S CASTLE

A RAMBLE ROUND THE
REALM OF CRICKET

IAN PEEBLES

Introduction by E. W. Swanton

THE PAVILION LIBRARY

First published in Great Britain 1958

First published in the Pavilion Library in 1986 by
Pavilion Books Limited
196 Shaftesbury Avenue, London WC2H 8JL
in association with Michael Joseph Limited
44 Bedford Square, London WC1B 3DU

British Library Cataloguing in Publication Data
Peebles, Ian
Batter's castle.
1. Cricket
I. Title
796.35'8   GV917

ISBN 1 85145 020 3
ISBN 1 85145 021 1 paperback

Printed and bound in Great Britain by
Billing & Sons Limited, Worcester

INTRODUCTION

One day in the spring of 1931 I made the journey from Fleet Street to Walham Green in London's western suburbs at the behest of my masters, the *Evening Standard*, in order to invite Ian Peebles to contribute a series of articles for us. There he was, one of the young white hopes of English cricket bowling away at Aubrey Faulkner's famous indoor School of Cricket, and there was I, an equally young and callow sporting journalist, charged with the job of persuading him to write a dozen pieces at the rate of fifteen guineas each. He mentioned the exact sum in his highly entertaining autobiography, *Spinner's Yarn*, and I'm sure he was correct for he never forgot a story or a significant personal fact, though the former with poetical licence he sometimes improved with a little judicious embroidery.

I did not find my sales-talk difficult, and, looking back, I am not surprised. For money went a longish way in the 'thirties, as I can recall if only because of two figures that stick in my mind. The fact was that Ian's fifteen guineas an article was £2 15s. more than I was paid weekly by the newspaper for my supposedly full-time services. Furthermore when, the following winter, we set ourselves up in bachelor residence, fifteen guineas *per month* was the exact rent we were charged by the retired barrister who was prepared to trust us with the occupation of his furnished rooms at 8 King's Bench Walk in the Temple.

We had not met before our business encounter at the cricket school, though I had watched, and reported on, the greatest of his achievements in his golden summer of 1930: the thirteen wickets for 237 in 81 overs in the University Match (despite which Oxford went down in the end to headlong defeat); his mastery, temporarily at least, of Don Bradman at Old Trafford (c. Duleepsinhji, b. Peebles 14); and his marathon six for 204 in the Oval Test. While Bradman was making hay and the one wicket apiece of Harold Larwood and Maurice Tate was costing a little matter of 285!

I must emphasise to the average reader of this new edition of

v

Batter's Castle – and only those far gone into the sere and yellow could have a first-hand memory of him in his prime, nor can it be detected from his charmingly modest writing – that for at least three seasons Ian Alexander Ross Peebles was a truly great leg-spin and googly bowler. Otherwise he would not have played in thirteen Test Matches for England at a moment in history when at least five other famous practitioners of the art, R. W. V. Robins and F. R. Brown (both high-class all-rounders), Richard Tyldesley, Tommy Mitchell and, above all, Tich Freeman were also at their peak.

Ian spun the ball enough, if not quite as sharply as some of this quintette. Where in his hey-day he had the advantage of all of them was in that precious, mysterious, elusive quality known as 'flight'. All too often the ball was not quite where the batsman thought it was. He played, mostly, a shade too early, or, sometimes, in a hurry – and not even those with the soundest techniques were proof against error. I am thinking now of his bowling on the plumb pitches typical of his time. When they had grown a bit dusty, and sometimes after rain, he could be a holy terror.

In 1929 – the unique year when the three Middlesex amateurs, he, Robins and Nigel Haig, all took 100 wickets – his bag was 123 at 19 apiece; in 1930 it was 133 at 18; in 1931 139 at 18. Those were the hey-day years, after which he developed persistent and painful trouble with his right shoulder and simultaneously 'lost' the spun leg-break. He could still roll it, and he could spin and turn the googly, and with his high, rhythmic, model action he remained a bowler to be reckoned with. But the magic that divided genius and utility had gone.

Aubrey Faulkner, with his wonderful flair as a teacher, had fashioned the talent that descended upon him in the shape of the raw youngster from Scotland. Ian was just eighteen when, in early 1926, he came south to work for Faulkner nominally as his secretary but principally to bowl, bowl and go on bowling to the clientele who thronged to his School. For a full two years, many hours a day, Ian followed the routine. In order to relieve his tiredness he even taught himself to bowl left-arm – I once in a match caught a slip catch from a quickish ball bowled with the wrong arm. It was the strain on those teenage shoulders which

built up a legacy of trouble. Though at first Ian remained
hopeful that time would do the trick, it never did. When he
captained Middlesex to second place in the Championship in
1939 he took 49 first-class wickets at 27 runs apiece. With that
action, and an ample supply of determination, he could never
be under-rated. But though he still derived much joy from all
that the game had to offer there was a melancholy underlying
feeling that his great potential had been only partially fulfilled.

It is time to move on from Ian's playing days to the literary
side of his cricket career, which covered the years from the end
of the war even beyond the publication of his autobiography in
1977 to a number of distinctive, perceptive biographies written
for *Barclays World of Cricket* during his last illness and within a
few months of his death in February, 1980.

To his regret the *Evening Standard* had failed to renew their
invitation to contribute in 1932, but there was just one slim
volume of a hundred pages which I remember for a literally
vivid reason. At the last moment the publishers of *How to Bowl*
wanted a picture of the famous arm at the point of delivery and,
the weather being inclement, Ian had to don a cricket shirt and
pose, rather unwillingly, in the sitting-room of 8 King's Bench
Walk. The photographer in far-off 1933 had to ignite a white
substance on a tray adjacent to the camera. The result was a
blinding flash, clouds of smoke billowing out of the windows
and the clattering arrival of the Temple fire-brigade. They were
not best pleased.

Ian was such a good talker and reminiscer, and had such an
individual turn of phrase that all the makings of a writer were
there, as *Everybody's* discovered, a magazine boasting at one
time a million circulation to which Ian managed to contribute
regularly, even when he was busily re-building, from small
pre-war beginnings, what became a highly prosperous wine
firm, which he ran in partnership with Hans Siegel. (This
charming man was the 'H.J.G.S., a non-cricketing but long
suffering business partner, entrapped in Batter's Castle these
twenty years' to whom he dedicated the first edition of this
book.) When one takes account of the fact that in this full
period of his life the budding wine-merchant's ardent courtship
of the ladies – over two decades! – culminated in 1947 in his

marrying Ursula Boxer (née Tulloch) and so taking on the responsibilities of family life, the evidence suggests that he really enjoyed writing, and indeed he did.

He became, in 1949, the *Sunday Graphic* cricket correspondent, and four years later was promoted within the Kemsley Group to the top cricket job on the *Sunday Times*. For them he covered the Australian visit of 1953 and England's recovery of The Ashes and the MCC tour of Australia in 1954–55 wherein we retained them. This was the first of three tours abroad, those to Australia in 1958–59 and to the West Indies in 1959–60 being the others. Increasingly Ian grew less happy at these long absences from family and business, and thereafter he confined himself to covering the home season, and to book-authorship, while much of the overseas reporting was undertaken for the *Sunday Times* by his old friend – and professional journalist – Jack Fingleton.

Ian was always an entertaining reporter, and his critical assessments of players and tactical situations were read with respect. The fact was, however, that his particular skill lay in the short essay – on any cricket subject, and especially one which allowed an outlet to his wit. Henry Longhurst, who for a while shared our Temple flat, and who was for many years Ian's colleague on the *Sunday Times* as golf correspondent, was likewise a master of the brief 'boxed' piece which Henry consciously kept to a length convenient for the golfer to absorb during his visit to the loo prior to the Sunday round. Ian and Henry formed a formidable pair both on and off the printed page.

In their company, the badinage passed to and fro at speed, and they made an even match. It isn't easy to put across the flavour of a 'genial insult' relationship among friends, but maybe this example will convey a hint of it. Henry was one day wearing a flag in his button-hole, and seeing Ian did not have one suggested in that unique, gravelly voice that so worthy a charity surely deserved some support even from a tight-fisted Scot. Ian promptly inspected the reverse side of Henry's flag and remarked laconically, 'As I thought – Press.'

All his books are lightened by anecdote, wherein as often as not the joke was on him. This one is typical enough. During the

Australians' visit to Oxford in 1930 Ian and a friend thought that a brief visit to the Pembroke College Ball would do no harm. The friend had a car, and they offered to drive a girl home. It turned out she lived not in Oxford but London. However, 'gallantry prevailed', and several hours later Ian in white tie and tails crept apprehensively into Brasenose with the dawn, absence overnight being a serious offence. To his dismay he found himself face to face with a don. 'Been to see the Pope?' he asked. Luckily perhaps, Dr McKie was a good Scot – but Ian had the sort of endearing personality that melted most people.

His biographies of famous contemporaries, Frank Woolley, Pat Hendren and Denis Compton, fondly written, are rich in first-hand reminiscence. His *Lord's (1946–1970)* written in collaboration with Diana Rait Kerr has a distinct historical value, as, of course, does *Spinner's Yarn*.

From the later 1950s the books flowed. This collection of essays was an early one, and it reflects Ian's cricket philosophy as well as any. The first edition was marred, by the way, only by his positively medieval indifference to spelling, an idiosyncrasy which no conscientious publisher should have allowed to go through unchecked. Happily the spelling mistakes have now been corrected, and *Batter's Castle* fully lives up to the general verdict on his writing of the late and great Lord Cobham: 'He writes about cricket beautifully and with knowledge, and above all wholly without rancour; Ian is sometimes critical but never unkind.' Charles Cobham would have greeted this reissue with the warmest approval.

E. W. Swanton, 1986

BATTER'S CASTLE

*A ramble round the realm
of cricket*

By IAN PEEBLES

With a Foreword by Peter May

CONTENTS

AROUND THE BATTLEMENTS

FOREWORD

A FURTHER OFFERING FROM THE PEN OF Ian Peebles is always an exciting event, and it is my great pleasure to produce the opening overs—even though bowling is something of a novelty for me.

Having spent a solitary winter at home and in the City, I should perhaps divulge that my office makes me an immediate neighbour of the author. In fact I am within an easy cricket ball's throw of his well-known firm of wine shippers where he spends his months of labour.

Ian is not only an authority on wine, he is also, as his friends will confirm, a delightful raconteur with a most vivid memory (for " useless information," as he modestly puts it) and I can assure you that he has given us many a laugh with his cricket reminiscences.

My one regret is that I did not have the pleasure of seeing Ian bowl when he was at his peak. We were lucky to have an insight into some of his mystery on the last tour of Australia when he gave us some much needed practice against this subtle form of spin—the rather unfortunate sequel was a broken finger which he was unwise enough to get in the way of a hard drive from one of the batsmen.

Finally, I do not feel it is necessary to recommend this book to you, because I am quite certain that it will be welcomed by cricket lovers everywhere, and I have no doubt that much enjoyment will be derived from it.

PETER MAY.

PREFACE

WHEN TOURING AUSTRALIA IN THE WAKE
of Sir Leonard Hutton's M.C.C. team I was fairly hard
worked. In addition to a good deal of newspaper work and
activity on other fronts I was writing a book about the
trip. As time pressed, in the latter pursuit, I had perforce
to spend many evenings at work and in consequence missed
many good parties.

There was one particular party which I was determined
to attend, at least for an hour or two, and this I did. But
at length the time came to go and I made my apologies
and explanations for my early departure. This did not
altogether please my hostess, a charming and forceful
Australian lady, whose knowledge of cricket was nil, and
who naturally had little patience with any literary work
on the subject.

" What are you going to call this blasted book of yours?"
she demanded. " Batter's Castle? "

For a moment I stood transfixed by this happy fluke of
feminine intuition.

" No," I said. " Not this one—but certainly the next."

Welcome, therefore, to Batter's Castle, a magic realm
open to anyone who has ever taken middle and leg in front
of it, or tried to bowl it down, or guarded it from the rear.
Or, indeed, to those who, for one reason or another, have
never themselves had such opportunity, but have delighted
in the progress of the active. Welcome also to the many
to whom the comparatively recently added Television
Portal and Wing have given limitless accommodation.

Within its battlements is the richest treasure house that
this particular inhabitant can imagine lying within the

11

grasp of the ordinary mortal. A brief inventory comprises the greatest active game yet devised, a truly democratic freemasonry, incomparable associations and memories, wit, fun, buffoonery, eccentricity, boundless character, disappointment and even heartbreak.

To the few it means fame, riches, travel and acquaintance with the great of the world. This does not, however, necessarily mean more bountiful reward than comes to the more humble who applaud and enjoy their success. The giants of the past have laid up their arms and devices and passed on, leaving a rich lore and many a good tale to be kept alive and embellished by other generations. These themselves are in turn constantly adding the fruit of their triumphs and disasters which will eventually become legend, even if, at this short distance, it is more difficult to recognise their true achievements.

In this book I have tried, however inadequately, to share some of the immense joy of one to whom Batter's Castle has been generous, indeed lavish. Apart from this endowment I can also claim to have been a member, at one time or another, of most degrees of its many estates; the player, the spectator, the official, the talker, the listener, the reporter and the would-be reformer. These pages are a fairly random collection of the thoughts, views, gossip and stories gathered in those various roles. I have also drawn upon pure imagination in including a couple of short stories, but even these are directly inspired by my memories of a particularly stout-hearted and lovable member of the Freemasonry, since departed the earthly castle, whose rich North Derbyshire accents still ring fondly in my ears.

CHAPTER ONE

The Game

"CRICKET IS A NOBLE GAME" WROTE PETER
Parley's Annual in 1840. " Do you know that even blood
royal has stood, bat in hand, surrounded by the young
buds of nobility? "

Indeed it is, but it is also the most democratic of sports.
For while the blood royal still stands bat in hand he is
likely, in modern times, to be surrounded by all manner of
humbler citizens. Presumably the only reservation is that,
under certain codes, not more than two may stand abaft
his leg stump at the moment the ball is bowled.

It seems that this sturdy democratic spirit has always
prevailed. One has but to cite the cavalier treatment of
King Edward VII who, as a young man in a much more
formal age, went forth to play cricket in Norfolk. The
score book reads " H.R.H. Prince of Wales b Wright o."
Apparently things were not so advanced, at least to English
eyes, in other countries. Through the mists of years there
drifts the memory of a cartoon in *Punch* during the first
war, depicting the Kaiser defending his wicket with a bat
which obscured all three stumps. The caption read:
" When the Kaiser plays what isn't cricket, God help the
Hun who takes his wicket." Some philosopher also said
that had the French nobility played cricket with their
tenantry, as did their English counterparts, there would
have been no revolution. This picturesque view is, to my
mind, open to question. It is surely more probable that
the combination of Latin temperament and body-line
bowling would have accelerated it.

Not that the ducal influence on the game has always been

13

as happy in this country as in the present age. It is recorded that the Duke of Cumberland, returned from the '45, made a match against the Earl of Winchilsea and, being a prudent man, " ordered twenty-two players to appear before him in order that he might pick the strongest side." Happily (I speak as half a Ross) his arrangements misfired and he found himself, like all selectors before or since, the subject of some opprobrium. The rejects took grave umbrage at what they considered his gross lack of judgment, and having challenged the favoured to a match at " a crown a head out of their own pocket," beat the daylights out of them. In this the royal selector may well have the sympathy of the M.C.C. Committee and their colleagues, if not of the clans but, as he also lost the main event, his critics seem to have been on firm ground.

One of the most touching tributes to the transcendent appeal of cricket came from an American friend. He arrived in this country for the first time in his life a few days before Christmas, but, in good American tradition, a party he would have. His circle of acquaintances though within its compass extremely varied was naturally small, so he invited them all. It was extremely unfortunate that two of the guests, a young scion of a noble house and the local newsvendor, should have embarked on the subject of politics as, while one evinced a true blue toryism, the other made no secret of his strong communist sympathies. When a deafening and most un-Yuletide row threatened to destroy the entire party the host made a despairing appeal. " For Pete's sake," he said, " can't you two guys talk of anything but politics? What about this weird game of yours, cricket or whatever it's called?"

The debaters paused and embarked on the suggested topic with due caution. But when it came to light that they were both fanatical Surrey supporters, a beautiful friendship was born and the party, my friend assures me, was the success of all time. He has now been in this country for several years, but has not yet actually seen a cricket match. In reflective moments, however, a reminiscent gleam comes into his eye and he opines that this cricket sure must have something.

How right he is—it sure has.

The Batsman

The Man
His Luck
His Bat
Chance of a Lifetime

The Batsman

And who like him could hand the bat
at this old English game.

THE FINE OLD ENGLISH CRICKETER.

CHAPTER TWO

The Man

THE BATSMAN IS, AS THE NAME OF THIS book implies, king of the castle. Although his life at all times hangs by a thread he can, so long as it is unbroken, savour the richest pleasure the game can offer. His success commands greater adulation than that of any other person. He is not the prime mover but he is the central figure in moments of ascendancy, the sun around which the satellites revolve, and in moments of stress the juicy bone over which his enemies snarl or scramble.

To achieve greatness the batsman must be blessed by nature with keen eyesight and sharp reflexes. Vital statistics do not seem to matter so are seldom recorded. But they vary between W.G.'s generous dimensions and the compact measurements of a Bradman. It is worthy of note, however, that amongst the truly great, the Champion is almost the only outsize. Indeed he complained slightly about this "all too solid flesh." Interviewed by the Strand Magazine in his glorious season of 1895 he was quoted as saying "Eighteen stone, for that is what I have weighed for many years past, is quite enough for me to carry when batting . . ."

It would be interesting to know if Warwick Armstrong had any similar comment to make for although not quite of the same calibre as a batsman he must rank as the leading batsman of avoirdupois amongst international batsmen. Despite strenuous spells in the stokehold of the good ship " Orontes " he took the crease in 1921 at around twenty-two stone. While on this fascinating tack, though the information is not available from the " Guinness Book of Records," it is a safe bet that Bonnor at six foot six was the loftiest Test match batsman and Willie Quaife the shortest. The temptation to proceed to the most portly and scrawniest must be eschewed as the subject then takes a rather personal turn, apart from the complication of seasonal variation.

All the great have been first-class technicians, which does not, of course, mean that they have been strictly orthodox. But there are certain immutable principles of batsmanship which must be observed by any human being however gifted in eye and reflex. Inevitably the name of Jessop will be raised in contradiction of this statement, but those who played with him say he observed these principles very shrewdly even if he applied them in a manner peculiar to his own genius. Certainly all the great I have seen were fundamentally sound. The quality common to all which put, or puts, them ahead of ordinary reliable performers is an immediate and early judgment of pace, length and direction which enables them to move into the most advantageous position immediately but without haste. Given this alacrity there is scope for various innovations beyond strictly orthodox practice and so is born the Compton sweep, Charlie Macartney's taste for late cutting half-volleys and full tosses and a variety of Don Bradman's more dazzling departures. George Gunn, characteristically, amused himself by occasionally applying the old-fashioned draw, a stroke which could seldom have been materially profitable, but did much to cheer or exasperate all present.

For lesser mortals there is seldom room for such embellishment and adherence to rule usually pays. One recalls Maurice Leyland's tale of the husky youngster at Headingley under the stern tutelage of Wilfred Rhodes. Having impressed on the novice the necessity of playing " leg and bat together " the great man bowled the appropriate ball to the off at which the pupil stretched a ponderous leg to mid-on and mowed the ball clean out of the ground. "Where's your leg?" demanded Wilfred.

" Never mind leg," replied the beaming striker, " look where bludy ball's gone."

The moral of this tale is that the applicant was not engaged.

By now I have seen a good many batsmen but I have never had reason to alter my opinion that, in all circumstances, Sir Jack Hobbs was the best of the lot. There was no troublesome bowler on any pitch whom he could not tackle more effectively than any rival. Pace, spin, swerve or googly he mastered with the same smooth ease. He brought much intelligence to bear on every situation and so applied his superb technique and natural ability to best advantage. He was not a killer by temperament and frequently, when the needs of his side were satisfied would give his wicket away. Sometimes his kindness misfired as he instanced the other day when we were talking of a dear friend of his, the rugged lovable Johnny Douglas. On the field Johnny gave no quarter and certainly asked for none, so when one day at Leyton he found himself opposed to Jack in best vein he exerted himself to the very limit. This availed him little until, sometime in the eighties, Jack snicked an outswinger so hard to the wicket-keeper that everyone heard it except the umpire who unhesitatingly said not out. The Colonel's rage was terrible to see (and hear) and he was still bowling like the east wind when the master completed his hundred. Having derived so much enjoyment from the last twenty, and perhaps moved by compassion for one so deserving, Jack then deliberately played all round a straight ball and was castled. The Colonel was somewhat mollified at what he described as " a little ruddy justice at last " and all would have been well if someone had not artlessly, or more probably artfully, pointed out that Jack had done this on purpose by way of compensation for his earlier luck. This set off an explosion which completely eclipsed the earlier slight contretemps and, so Jack avers, far outshone his own modest efforts in sheer entertainment value. It might

have lessened the outraged bowler's blood pressure to
reflect that his would-be benefactor always regards him as
the best he knew with the new ball.

At 76 The Master is a sprightly young man of most
disarming, boyish humour. Despite the grandeur of his
career, amongst his happiest memories he still recalls the
great cap incident at the Lord's Test Match in 1930. This
occurred largely because Greville Stevens had told Walter
Robins to nobble him an England cap as his own was
worn out or lost, and Walter obligingly put an extra one
in his bag. But when the time came it was discovered
that *all* the new caps had mysteriously disappeared where-
upon there was a great hue and cry and the Chairman of
Selectors, Henry Leveson Gower, was much exasperated
and decreed all bags must be searched. This was exceedingly embarrassing for Walter who was aware he had one
surplus to requirements. His embarrassment was considerably increased when, in the midst of an accusing
silence no less than twelve caps were extracted from the
lining of his bag. None looked more self-righteous during
this operation than Jack who, having heard of Walter's
generosity towards his colleague, had spent a happy ten
minutes stuffing them into the bag, while its owner battled
with Clarrie Grimmett in the middle.

To pick a post-war counterpart of Hobbs is a ticklish
question. In the last ten years there have come to light a
number of superb batsmen but none who gives quite
the same impression of complete self-sufficiency—so far.
Compton, Hutton, May, Worrell, Walcott, Weekes have
all made the highest grade.

Bradman one must exclude as a post-war figure as his
overlap was small and his golden era pre-war. Peter May
is the best player in the game at the moment and at 28 has
already created a very remarkable record. It must be
remembered that a large proportion of his runs have been
made on pitches far inferior to the beauties of the pre-war
days where runs flowed smoothly from bowling which
could achieve neither turn nor pace from a placid over-

prepared surface. On such pitches even the new ball was shorn of its dangers by lack of life and when the shine was gone the bowler was left to rely on faith and hope, charity being at a discount in the circumstances. In recent years both in Australia and this country the batsman has had to cope with very different conditions in which the new ball has come quickly at differing heights and the old one has started to turn early in the proceedings. Occasionally when a puff of dust has gone up on the first day of a Test Match I have stolen a look at Bill O'Reilly, half expecting to see a silent tear trickle into his typewriter as he thought of the Oval in 1938. But that splendid, and very Australian, soul has always been happily absorbed in his literary fulminations, attacking the machine as he used to run up after being hit for four, seemingly forgetful of the days when he described his lot as that of a galley slave.

The point is that May has had to battle for all his runs and mostly in the knowledge that his side's fortunes depended heavily upon his success. Additionally he now carries the immense responsibilities of a Test match captain. He has, however, the ideal temperament to carry these burdens being a young man of quite remarkably sound sense and determination. With years before him he may well become one of the major legends in the Atomic Age, when it is to be hoped cricket will still be played in its present form and not by some press-button process.

On the subject of the greatest many will wonder why I do not put Bradman first. As I have written before I would unhesitatingly put him first on hard wickets but because he was vulnerable on soft patches, whatever the reasons, he must, at least in my opinion, take second place to Hobbs who excelled on them. Bradman on fast wickets was certainly most dazzling and entertaining and entirely unique in his complete range of strokes, devastating power and immense stamina. In post-war days only Denis Compton, in a vastly different vein, has rivalled the great Bradman's onslaughts of the thirties. Where Bradman bore an air of ruthless efficiency, Compton at all times seemed to exude good nature and enjoyment. Their respective performances between the wickets were plainly indicative of their differing approaches to the business in hand. Where one ran swiftly and purposefully, weighing every factor of speed and turn, the other would set off light heartedly as a man on a pleasant country ramble, without previous reference to the barometer. The not infrequent confusion resulting from the latter method lent a fine gusto to the proceedings and only the churlish would count the cost in nervous wear and tear.

In passing it may be said on Denis' behalf that he was brought up in a very eccentric school of runners, for Middlesex have always been extremely unpredictable in this department. The reason for this is obscure. It can hardly be argued that the slope at Lord's is responsible, being very gentle, and in any case in the wrong direction. It could hardly be the disparity in speed and braking power between Joe Hulme the Arsenal flyer and behemoths like Durston and Smith, for the complaint goes back further. At any rate in my time no Middlesex innings was without incident at some point.

Of all the impetuous in those happy days who rushed madly to and fro with or without co-operation from the other striker, the most spectacular was undoubtedly Tom Enthoven, one of the greatest of Middlesex characters. Elsewhere I have quoted the legend of his term's captaincy of Cambridge. Briefly it was said that he ran his entire side out once and would easily have done so twice but for the saving clause that every time he awarded a " blue " the grateful recipient thenceforward refused to run except on his own and less enterprising terms. Tom's taste for adventure seemed to increase with the years and with time he developed another somewhat disconcerting habit. On turning after every run he would make a wide hairpin bend away from the wicket, so that he would wind up miles from the starting point thus greatly complicating the umpire's calculations. According to eye witnesses in an early season match played near the Tavern, he ran a four on the last lap, went belting along the rails urged on by friendly slaps on the back from the spectators, with a despairing umpire taking a sighter on hands and knees.

These memories were vividly recorded for me when the other day we met, as we occasionally do for lunch, and Tom related how he had just played in a parents v. school match and taken part in a great stand. The feature of the partnership from his point of view was the smooth, almost machine-like running between the wickets. His calls were immediately and decisively answered and he was congratulating himself on his uncanny judgment when at a late stage the ball was hit for four and his partner paused to address him as they met in mid-wicket.

"Don't bother to call," he said. "I'm absolutely stone deaf."

The batsman, when he reaches a certain level, is a public entertainer. In fact he is the leading attraction to the spectator, for while many bowlers have had their followers it is the magic name of Bradman or Hammond or Hutton which draws the major portion of the crowds. It is natural, therefore, that the follower looks for more than mere effectiveness in his hero's performances. In the very nature of the game grace of execution has always ranked high in the connoisseur's scale of virtues, thus, although Frank Woolley has a variable record in the very highest class of cricket, his place amongst the great is assured. His appearance at the pavilion gate, especially in his native Kent, was an almost dramatic moment, the tall majestic figure striding unhurried and competent midst the ecstatic clamour of all good Kentish men and men of Kent, to say nothing of their feminine counterparts. When we as young and enthusiastic bowlers had got a couple of quick wickets Pat Hendren would bring us down with a bump.

"Here he comes," he would say with malicious glee. "The Lion Tamer."

Later I comment on the beauty of a cricket bat as an

implement, but no one can ever put it to more consistently graceful use than Frank Woolley. In recent years a christian namesake, Frank Worrell, has produced his strokes with a fluid ease seldom bettered but perhaps lacking quite the effortless power which caused the ball, to paraphrase Neville Cardus, to make a more beautiful curve when struck by Woolley than when struck by anyone else. Tom Graveney when under way is the most graceful of modern batsmen but Ian Craig, although he lacks the height which makes for the deceptively placid swing, is as good-looking a player as one could see.

If not perhaps in the best of taste, it is nigh irresistible to speculate on the opposite end of the scale, and here the redoubtable Kenny Mackay must be a strong candidate, for supremacy or the reverse. It is somewhat strange, for the prodding, pawky, pushing method of batting is in sharp contrast to a pleasant rhythmic bowling action. As an opponent he must have a high irritation value with more movement in his steadily champing jaws than in his bat. In this respect he has bettered Mr. Gladstone's maxim of 30 chews to the bite by about 100 to 1.

The really worthwhile distinction of the worst batsman must go to South Africa where Alfie Hall, medium-quick left-hand, bowled magnificently but seldom connected with his limited range of strokes. I have heard his fellow left-hander Bert Ironmonger of Australia named for this honour, but not having seen him in action am prepared to elect Alfie without calling further evidence. This is generous, for he once hit me for four in a Test Match at Johannesburg, and the crowd cheered for five minutes without drawing breath.

In the post-war era there have been several international left-handers of top class, but England failed to produce a really successful one until the arrival of Richardson. This has been a considerable want for some time, for the left-hander has a value beyond his material worth. The very change in focus and field is a distraction and many bowlers are disarmed by reason of their type or temperament. In pre-war days Maurice Leyland was the strongest stabilising factor in England's batting order and it is splendid to see that Richardson has the same battling spirit. In fact, Richardson to the ordinary observer is mostly defence and indomitable spirit. In the course of one of his less convincing innings someone observed to an old-timer that he looked rather bad and received the devastating reply that he hadn't got enough strokes to be bad.

That, however good as a turn of phrase, is far from truth as a judgment. Richardson is an eminently sensible young man and jests quite happily about his strokes, numbers one, two and three, and the fact that any further enterprise brings on his head the good-natured wrath of Captain and Chairman. The real fact of the matter is that he knows his powers and limitations to a tee when opposed by Test Match bowling and applies or avoids them accordingly. The results are plain to see. One is that he has reached 1,000 runs in Test Match cricket sooner than any other batsman.

It is strange that New Zealand, with their comparatively small share of the cricketing population, have produced the two most attractive left-handers of the present decade. Martin Donnelly was not only the most attractive but the best left-hander for many a day. A sound defence and a wonderful range of strokes were allied to the most sunny and equable temperament you could find from Bramall Lane to Wanganui. Lloyd George said there was only one thing wrong with the Scots, there weren't enough of them. The same charge could be brought against Donnelly—there just wasn't enough of him. A war with the New Zealand Division and business and family matters meant but a short cricket career. He is now very much a business and family man and lives, appropriately enough, in McCartney Avenue.

His fellow countryman, Sutcliffe, promised to outshine any rival when he first came to this country, but does not so far seem to have fully realised these potential powers. However, by the time these words are printed he may well have refuted them.

Few modern batsmen have given me more pleasure than Arthur Morris. There was a thumping power and crispness about his handling of the bat that gave every stroke character and the whole performance a dominating air. Where he rates amongst the top class is difficult to decide, for there were certain inherent weaknesses in his defence which came to light when hard pressed. One was a tendency to play from crease and so give the ball just room enough to find the edge or beat the bat when it moved. Another was an apparent difficulty in plotting his position in regard to his leg stump which resulted in his being bowled behind his legs more than any other player within living memory. In his last appearance against Surrey at the Oval he was going very well when once again his old enemy Alec Bedser caught him out of position and knocked his leg stump down. At that Dick Whitington heaved a great sigh. "A moment ago," he said, " I sent a cable 13,000 miles to say that Morris has cured this weakness and was never now bowled round his legs."

A little later we took the field together for the Forty Club at Eton. We all wanted to see Arthur get a few as it would have been a great treat for friend and foe alike, and as he went I said, without thought of any real danger, " For Pete's sake, mind that leg stump." To which he replied, " Don't worry—it never happens any more." Perhaps between us we had tempted the Fates for, third over, a very young bowler emulated Alec Bedser by hitting both middle and leg.

In passing I may say that my own innings in this match did much to compensate for this disappointment. With Arthur's failure it came to a very tight finish and as I sat waiting to bat number eleven very few runs separated us. Our captain generously offered to lay me three to one that I wouldn't get off the mark, which I took for a modest sum. A moment later he was back to apologise for being so stingy, saying that they were laying ten to one further down the line. At that moment the ninth wicket fell, two or three were needed, and I went to join Jack Young, going in at the non-striker's end. We had a real Middlesex finish. Jack hit the ball to mid wicket and called " Two," and I had covered about one and two-fifths of the required distance when he suddenly said " No." The immediate result of this denial was that I pulled both Achilles tendons, fell flat on my face and was run out by a yard, so losing the match and my bet. There was great hilarity at this, but none laughed more heartily than Dr. Birley, the head-master, who had heard the preliminaries and left the scene with difficulty.

Neil Harvey is a glorious player to see on fast wickets, but has had a lean time against England for the most part of the last three or four series. There is an element of ill luck attached to this, for the mind's eye can see him on several occasions getting impossibly good balls or being snapped up by some abnormally agile fieldsman. But in his case again there is a very definite suspicion of risk in the way he plays the moving or turning ball. Against other Dominions, who play on absolutely plumb fast wickets, his record is splendid, and if Australian wickets are up to pre-war standards this next winter he will be a very big problem to our bowlers. Having started so young he should have years of cricket ahead of him.

Youth is powerfully on the side of Sobers, the latest recruit to the left-handed brigade of international calibre. He was the one new arrival with the last West Indies team who fulfilled his reputation and showed a good resource-ful courage when things were going wrong, as they fre-quently were. He is not only a very good player but an exceedingly attractive one, with a flowing grace which must inevitably be compared with that of Woolley. To me any batsman who makes three hundred runs is a bore, but if I had to see any present-day player do so I would as soon have Sobers as any other. His record score was made in ten hours, which is three hours improvement on Sir Leonard and no less than six on Hanif.

In thirty years the changes in the technique of the batsman have been very small, and chiefly confined to personal idiosyncrasies. There have, however, been considerable changes in tactics which have been dictated by alterations in the laws and different methods of attack. Broadly speaking, the centre of gravity has shifted so that in modern times there is a much greater emphasis on leg side play. Several factors have contributed to this.

The new lbw rule certainly had some influence in this direction but, to my way of thinking, less than is generally supposed. At least it has to some extent diminished the blatant injustice of the batsman being empowered to ignore any ball of doubtful quality or intention outside the off stump. As long as the clause relating to the legs being in line between wicket and wicket is retained this privilege will persist to a degree, as the batsman can still use his front leg with almost complete impunity. The fast bowler can anyway console himself with the thought that he can now get an lbw decision with a good length ball, a feat which was geometrically impossible under the old rule, if his action was high.

With so little encouragement to the off it is not altogether surprising that the bowler has tried the other side, and this with great success—such success that it has become necessary to limit his activities by restricting his leg side field. It does not, however, make for the most attractive cricket, but it does ensure that the modern batsman must be a competent and extremely vigilant on side player in order to succeed. No longer is the region from fine leg to deep square a safety zone for beautiful thrusting and deflecting strokes off the pads, but a certain death trap for the unwary.

What does strike one is that with the off spinner so much to the fore the batsman does not more frequently advance to the attack. The off spinner has less answer to this treatment than the leg spinner who can always give the ball a bit more width. Having discussed this with several of our best batsmen I have received much convincing argument as to why this is so infrequent. They point out that all the good off spinners, Tayfield, Laker, etc., are just of a pace where it is very hard to get to them and that they can always speed up a shade if necessary. Further, unless one can clear the ring consistently, there is a limited area in which to place the ball. Modern in-fielders are quite liable to freeze on to a full-blooded drive from very short range. The middle distance is well populated to the on and to retreat and hit the ball on the off is always fraught with hazard. Personally I am prepared to sympathise with these views for, as anyone who has been through the mill will agree, things have a habit of looking vastly different in the middle.

There, then, is a brief glimpse of the batsman within his realm.

CHAPTER THREE

His Luck

BATSMEN, BEING AFTER ALL HUMAN BEINGS, are very variable in temperament and approach to the job. Some are phlegmatic, some highly strung, some are even superstitious. Many, without being exactly superstitious, have their foibles and customs which lend them comfort. Sir Pelham Warner was so attached to his Harlequin cap that it became almost a national emblem, like W. G.'s beard. Denis Compton always liked his partner to walk out on his left and not to change places on his way to the crease. Trevor Bailey likes to take a book to the ground, not only for the improvement of his mind, but because it has always brought him ill luck if he has not. For years of his life Wally Hammond used to bat with sleeves buttoned down to his wrists, but, whether for greater comfort or due to change of faith, he eventually always rolled them up. Jack Robertson of Middlesex and England always put his cap on as soon as he started to change. He was preceded in this by Arthur Shrewsbury of yesteryear, but in the case of the old master it may have had some connexion with his very bald pate, a feature on which he was acutely sensitive. At any rate, it was said he would pop his head into his shirt with a bowler hat on it and pop it out crowned by his Notts cap.

But no habit or totem meant anything to Victor Trumper who said that there was no such thing as luck. Well, with his genius and generous philosophical temperament he may well have been able to ignore Fortune's blandishments and rise above her churlishness but few, especially of lesser calibre, would deny that there is a whale of a lot of luck in cricket.

32

There have been players who were famously or notoriously lucky, according to which side you happened to be on. F. S. Jackson won all five tosses when he captained England in 1905. Herbie Collins won most of his when he led Australia, and his general good fortune was such that he was nicknamed " Horseshoe." In his tale of his trip to Australia, Cecil Perkin says that while they used to say of David Denton, " Who's going to miss him? " of Herbie Collins they would say, " Who, if anyone, is going to catch him? "

It is fair to say that the old saw " Fortune smiles on the brave " is peculiarly true to cricket. Take the case of Herbert Sutcliffe, also regarded as having a maddeningly lucky star. True, he seemed to play on without removing the bails, put more catches between fielders, and be dropped more than most, but perhaps that was because he stayed longer at the crease than most. At any rate, no menace perturbed him, and he remained unmoved by the sighs of fielders and the curses of bowlers.

I remember walking out at Bradford with Pat Hendren who, seeing Herbert behind us, rashly said, " He's out of luck this season—they don't drop him any more." No? At 2, mid-on grounded a sitter, and when he was 7 I bowled him a leg-break which he tickled to Pat at first slip, where a miracle occurred and that went to the floor too. We didn't see any further mistake, but we did see another 182 runs of the highest quality.

Talking of Pat Hendren, he once struck a patch of bad luck which can seldom, if ever, have been equalled. It was back in the late 'twenties and, when it got to July, he had hardly made a run. The climax came when he went to leave a ball from Sam Staples two feet outside the off stump. It pitched in a hole from the previous match next door, shot up in the air, and hit the knob of the upheld bat handle. From there it shot into the stumps, the whole effect being reminiscent of a display of trick billiards at Thurston's Hall. Next time out, Pat decided to have a bang, and, from then on, broke all records.

This wrestle with the Gods of Chance had, I suspect, a sinister sequel. In 1934 Don Bradman, out of form and out of luck, took guard at Lord's against Middlesex at 25 minutes to 6. The first two balls from Jim Smith missed the edge of the bat by a fraction, and Don smiled disconsolately at the slips. "What does a chap do when he's plumb out of luck?" he asked.

"Have a bang," replied the warm-hearted Pat.

By half-past six the "bang" had become a hundred and, after that, Don never looked back.

So there you have good luck and bad luck, but there's still another kind of luck, typified by one of my favourite old and true cricket stories.

Long ago, a visiting fast bowler found himself, late at night, in the opposition camp without any place to lay his head. All the pubs were full, so at last he sought the hospitality of his old friend, the home team's opening batsman, a good and Christian man, who bade him welcome. Accommodation was so limited that a new arrival meant quite a bit of reorganisation, but eventually host and guest bedded down together in the spare room.

Now the host, as I have said, was a devout man, so before retiring he prayed, in rather indiscreetly powerful tones, that the morrow might bring him a hundred at the expense of the visiting team. The visitor listened to this appeal with wonderment and growing alarm and, though unpractised in such devotions, felt something should be done to counter this unpredictable advantage. The moment his friend had done, he raised his own voice and, imitating so far as he could his host's reverent phrases, prayed that he might shatter him for nowt.

The strained amosphere resulting from this spiritual competition was much aggravated on the following day when the bowler's first delivery sent the batsman's middle stump cartwheeling out of the ground. The batsman took this very much to heart, considering he had been completely out-supplicated by a novice. The more cynical were probably nearer the truth, however, when they dismissed the whole incident as merely another case of beginner's luck.

Sometimes, of course, superstition is confounded, and here is a tale with a moral. Percy Sherwell and Bill Shalders of the South African side set out to the Lord's Test Match of 1907 together. On their way they met a sweep and Shalders raised his hat and, bowing, said " Good morning, Mr. Sweep." What the sweep said is not recorded, but Sherwell said " Aw, nuts," or whatever was the current equivalent. The final answer was supplied by next morning's papers which read " W. A. SHALDERS b HIRST o. P. W. SHERWELL b BLYTHE 115."

This moral I can endorse by a painful personal memory. In days before nationalisation there was a fleet of coal trucks on the Great Western Railway rejoicing in the name Jud Bud and, in my university days, it was considered very good luck to see one, provided one observed the ceremony, which was exactly the greeting accorded to a sweep except for the change of title. In 1939, when captaining Middlesex, I was travelling from Oxford to London on the Friday evening before the Yorkshire match when out of the window I espied a shining new Jud Bud. There was too much at stake to take any risks so, despite a fairly crowded compartment, I gave it the traditional " Good morning, Mr. Jud Bud " in loud firm tones. The atmosphere in the carriage for the rest of the journey was that of visiting day at Broadmoor, but I suffered this embarrassment cheerfully in view of the great things to come. They came. I lost the toss, dropped a sitter, and Yorkshire, aided by several other drops, batted all day on a beauty. It rained profusely over the week-end and we batted twice on a lovely sticky wicket. The only worse time I can recall was when one of the Temple pigeons landed a full toss on the crown of my hat.

Never mind, Mr. Jud Bud has been obliterated so can no longer entrap the trusting. Pigeons, on the other hand, are still active. But I can warn you—they *ain't* lucky.

CHAPTER FOUR

His Bat

PRESUMABLY EVERY SPORTSMAN OR GAMES player considers the implements of his own craft the most beautiful man-made objects in the world. A tennis racket, a gun, a rod or a lacrosse stick has a special magic for some hand or eye. Even a boxing glove has its beauty—if not in the eye of the beholder.

To the batsman there is, of course, no implement more beautiful than his bat, whether in the dazzling bloom of its youth or in the nobbly sweetness of its old age. In its youth it can probably claim priority of place in any beauty competition of sporting goods, even to the untutored eye. Its perfect complexion, its balance, its symmetry, the confluent curves like the hull of a clipper, and, engraved on its brow, the name of your favourite batsman, amateur or professional. No wonder the shopper, old or young, astigmatic, dropsical or even an habitual number eleven, automatically picks up this splendid weapon and defiantly addresses himself to an imaginary Lindwall, about to attack him from the ladies' underwear end.

The bat has taken quite some time to reach its present shape and form, for the stages of its evolution have been fairly lengthy. Its patriarch was doubtless the monks' crick or staff which was primarily designed to aid its owner's progress by guiding his footsteps or cracking the skull of the footpad. It is unlikely that there was any great alteration in its design when some jolly Abbot discovered that it was great fun to have a Brother roll a stone for him to bat away. The game had reached a much more formal stage when the oldest surviving bat was fabricated, but as the bowling with which it had to contend was still along the ground, the business part of the blade was an arc at the end, giving it the appearance of a ponderous hockey stick.

In the 1770s the effect of length bowling was being felt, and by 1773 John Small (of "pitch a wicket, play at cricket" fame) had produced a straight-bladed bat with shoulders. It was in the following year that there occurred on the Hambledon ground a scene which was to have a lasting influence on the future of the cricket bat.

At a crucial moment in the match between Hambledon and Ryegate a gentleman of the Runyonesque name of "Shock" White took guard with an immense bat which covered the entire wicket. There being no legislation on the point the Hambledonians took direct action and chopped this monstrosity down to more reasonable proportions on the spot. Apparently they didn't chop quite enough for White won the match for his side, but at least they had brought to light the pressing need for some regulation regarding the size of the bat. Very soon afterwards the maximum width of the blade was limited to four and a quarter inches, a limitation which has remained unchanged to this day. So far as I know the only suggestion of any alteration came comparatively recently from Walter Robins, who advocated a smaller bat to counter inflated scoring. When, on his next appearance at Lord's, he made a sharp nought there was great ribaldry and a chorus of enquiries as to the size and nature of the bat he carried to and from the wicket, unmarked.

The present shape and size of the bat seems to have been standardised about 1827, and this was again due to a bowling development. It was in this year that Lillywhite and Broadbridge of Sussex began the era of genuine round arm bowling, and in so doing, vastly changed the technique of batting. The bat was now similar in frontal elevation to its modern counterpart, but made all in one piece and without the bulge behind. It was nonetheless heavier, with stout durable edges, but the lack of insulation due to its

one-piece construction must have been painfully apparent
to the user whose timing was at fault on a chilly May day.

The cane handle was introduced in 1840 and was the
greatest single advance in the whole progress of bat
making. There has, in fact, been no major innovation with
the exception of the bulge which appeared in the 'nineties.

Even without this embellishment the bats of the nine-
teenth century must have been lusty affairs. One has but
to think of George Parr thrashing the ball over his favourite
tree (still happily preserved) or Bonnor almost preceding
the Sputnik by seventy years. The Rev. W. Fellowes, who
drove the ball 175 yards from hit to pitch whilst at practice
on the Christchurch ground at Oxford, must have, apart
from the merits of his wood, struck a very good ball, for
they also vary in their resilience. Mr. William Ward, the
immortal saviour of Lord's, wielded a bat weighing four
pounds, a weight lifter's number in the eyes of the modern
player who prefers something between two pounds two
and two pounds four ounces.

W. G., to judge from photographs and an example
preserved at Lord's, used bats in keeping with his impressive forearms. In his interview with the representative of
the *Strand* magazine, in which he complains of his own
weight, he has nothing to say about that of his bat. Indeed,
although he touches on practically every aspect of the
game, he has singularly little to say on this important
subject. "And now for the bat. No doubt you have
observed the peculiarity of many players in respect of the
length of the handle. Some have long, others again have
shorter. I myself prefer a handle of the ordinary length,
and hold it half way up." On the lower and more interesting portion he has no comment to make, but, with his usual
profound common sense, he has a word on its proper
application. "Then you must make the bat hit the ball,
not let the ball hit the bat."

Prince Ranjitsinhji, in *The Jubilee Book*, is much
more explicit regarding the qualities to be sought in
choosing a bat. Having dwelt for some time on the evils of

a bat which is unsuitable for size or weight, he says, " The wood of which cricket bats are made may be divided according to colour. There are intermediate shades but most bats are either white or red." He explains the merits of each type, pointing out that the white is sweeter but the red more durable and requiring more use to reach its best. But, despite the increased need for economy, fashion over the years has decreed that white is the popular colour and, in modern times, a red wood bat is almost unknown, whatever its practical advantages.

The cult of the "Autographed" bat was started by Messrs. Gunn and Moore with their famous brand of that name, the quality of which was endorsed by a facsimile of William Gunn's signature. The practice spread but slowly, but, in the early years of the century, J. T. Tyldesley was signing his name on the products of Tyldesley and Holbrook of Manchester. It was in post First War days that the practice became widespread. Sir Jack Hobbs lent his name to the " Force " bat and by 1939 every maker of note had almost every player of note contracted to endorse his wares. Twenty years later some firms have several prominent names attached to their different brands. Whether a famous name does anything for the quality of a bat I doubt, but I do still recall the thrill of the name " Jack Hobbs " stamped on a bat bought forty years ago.

Apart from the intrinsic merits of the bat a great deal, rather obviously, depends upon the use, even amongst the great. Aubrey Faulkner had an illustrative story. When in Australia with the South African team he went to call on Victor Trumper in his sports store. Trumper was no sort of salesman for, his nature being as generous as his bat, he much preferred to give things away. Sure enough he presented Aubrey with a bat which the recipient promptly used against the donor's side, New South Wales. The results were disappointing and, when asked, Faulkner had in honesty to say that the present was hard and unpleasant. Trumper was much concerned at this but, picking up the offending bat, gave the handle a few wiggles with his steel-like wrists, and said he would take it in with him. Aubrey said he could hardly recognise it as the same bat when the ball flew from it with a mellow " ponk." At the end of the day he got it back again with an assurance that it was all right, but in fact found no difference. Allowing for the modesty of a good man, one may say that it just goes to show.

One of the most perfect of bats was made about this time by Gunn and Moore, and remains in their possession as a model. It belonged to the late " Pete " Perrin who made over 2,000 runs with it. It weighs well, two pounds and several ounces, but is so beautifully balanced that it comes up like a feather. Right over the middle of the bulge there is a gentle scoop which is a great credit to its owner, for the rest of the blade is unmarked. This perfection may well have influenced Pete, a man of pawky wit, for when asked his opinion of a bat of lesser breed he remarked that it should make a nice couple of pipes.

It is difficult to imagine a more perfect tool for the job than the orthodox bat, but there have been attempts at improvement in its performance and construction. Don Bradman at one time experimented with a steel-handled bat but it never reached the stage of general production. Curiously enough, the only other experimenter in this direction seems to have been his fellow countryman, one Mayor Tunks, who used an iron-handled bat in New South Wales over a century ago.

What promised to be a sound and economical idea was a laminated blade, suggested, I believe, by Herbie Taylor. This was to be constructed by bonding strips of willow together instead of carving from the solid. Whether this scheme met with any success or not I do not know, but it might well be worth re-investigating in view of the enormous advance in bonding agents in recent years. Nor can I say if any patent rights are involved, but it might be a bet for some enterprising maker.

There have been plenty of freak bats. One legendary model was variable in weight, the alteration being effected by a round block of wood which screwed into its bustle. In modern times Jim Smith, loftiest and lengthiest of all hitters and the only man whose appearance regularly emptied the Tavern and Long Bar, had one or two pretty impressive bats. They were something between a blunderbuss and a ship of the line, with a special long handle and a good weight of willow, a fitting instrument for their owner's six foot five and eighteen stone. One day, against Hants, he hit Alec Kennedy so high that, in addition to our running two runs before it descended and mid-off being ruined when it did, the concussion was such that this mighty blade was riven from splice to oil hole. A replacement was dragged forth by the twelfth man and out of curiosity I went to pick it up. The effort required to raise the normal bat made no impression on this outsize and, much awed, I said to Jim, " With this you ought to clear the river." But the owner wasn't convinced. After a few speculative waggles he shook his head. " No good," he said. " No wood in it."

The maker of this splendid thing, Stuart Surridge, knows as much about bats as any living man. He makes them, uses them and loves them, and on entering a cricket ground he can tell at a glance any batsman using one of his. In his showrooms he has the finest collection of historic bats which I have ever seen, all made by three generations of his family. Probably pride of place is given to one used by W. G., and signed by him across the face. It is a truly noble object, deep mahogany in colour, with lots of wood but beautifully manageable. Apparently old bats dry out with age, so that this one is a good deal lighter than when the Champion thrust it massively at the best the Players could bring against him.

The names of the other users read like a history of cricket—Fry, Hayward, A. O. Jones, Noble, Ranji, Crawford, Faulkner, Hobbs, Sutcliffe, Hammond, Duleep, and May. Amongst scores of others there is one of Jim Smith's, but it is not so massive as my memory of the model quoted above. Perhaps my recollection has grown fonder with the years or perhaps Jim grew refined in his later days.

Wally Hammond's bat was interesting in that he liked a fairly heavy bat, by modern standards, and he liked the weight fairly low in the blade, which one was always told did not make for good balance. His record breaking bat has this club-like character to a marked degree. In discussing these matters apparently Wally very shrewdly remarked that once you had got the bat up, for which there is plenty time, the added weight low down is of considerable advantage. The results certainly bore this out.

Surridge is of the opinion that the top class players had few fads about their bats, once satisfied as to weight, balance and sweetness. The average run about two pounds four ounces and are usually pressed rather lighter than those sold to the club player, who is likely to encounter rather harder balls and wants a bat which will last well. That which Duleep used in his prime is hardly pressed at all so that, whilst it must have been as sweet as honey, it is covered with a myriad of little cracks all over the surface of the operative part.

Peter May, although six feet tall, likes a short handle, and having started with very light bats has grown progressively heavier in his taste, so that the present range scale a little over two pounds five ounces. He always likes to have a couple at concert pitch so alike as to be completely interchangeable. Peter Richardson, on the other hand, uses the lightest practical weight, about two pounds one ounce.

The bat, like its user, is a wide subject but, also like its user, has changed fundamentally not at all in the last generation. It is still, in a machine age, the work of a craftsman and here, in conclusion, is a tale illustrative of his skill. In pre-war days Surridges supplied a bat to "Sonny" Avery, the Essex batsman, which he used against Surrey at the Oval to make a very respectable score. He was delighted with it, but complained that it sounded as though it were hollow and, the factory being handy, he brought it in for examination. The cause of this peculiarity was soon discovered. A tap with a mallet parted handle and blade cleanly and immediately; by an oversight they had never been glued together but, so perfect was the fit, it had stayed put through his innings and might have done so indefinitely.

It seems to me that there is but one improvement an article of this quality calls for—the removal of the purchase tax.

CHAPTER FIVE

Chance of a Lifetime

I ALWAYS ENJOYED BATTING AGAINST Yorkshire. The standard of bowling and fielding was of the best, just the thing to test the ambitious player, and Arthur Wood behind the stumps was splendid company. What's more, it is always nice to know that one is welcome, and the Yorkshiremen were always so unaffectedly delighted to see me at the crease that it gave me a nice warm glow —just like the arrival of the Sunday joint. Further, it is an axiom in the entertainment world that the show should end with the customer wanting more, and for my part I was a good guest, never outstaying my welcome.

While thumbing through *Wisden* the other day I came on a notable example of those happy occasions. It was the M.C.C. v. Yorkshire match of 1936, and there were two unusual features which had quite a bearing on the match, at least so far as I was concerned. The first was that the Senior Club, exercising its prior right, enlisted the services of Bill Bowes so that he was playing against his own county. The second was that Brian Sellers, as the only visiting amateur, was asked to change in our dressing room, this being before the democratic days when all scrum in together.

Now whatever he may say to the contrary, Bill Bowes, when it came to batting, just wasn't in the same class as myself. Our captain seemed to be clear on this point for, having nominated the first six strikers, he unhesitatingly wrote my name at number ten and Bill's at number eleven. The coughing, whistling and raising of eyebrows with which number eleven greeted his decision struck me as

44

being in very poor taste. Our captain also fell abruptly
in my estimation when he responded to these gestures by
saying he didn't care a rap which way we went in. However, as the score card was printed in that order we
eventually stuck to it.

It had been my intention to assert my superiority on this
occasion for good and all, but owing to circumstances
beyond my control, to wit a ball of smart pace from Mr.
Smailes and the capacious gloves and stentorian baritone
of Mr. Wood, it turned out that Bill and I made identical
scores. So identical, in fact, that had Bill, a king mathe-
matician, multiplied our scores together, divided one by
other or subtracted the first from the second and squared
the result, the answer would have been the same in every
case.

Such was the disappointment of this reverse that I
gracefully suggested that Bill should precede me in the
second innings, an invitation which he duly accepted. It
didn't avail him much, as in the second innings our eighth
wicket fell at 25 past six, so he had to scuffle in as night
watchman but survived to be 0 not out overnight.

Next morning broke a beautiful day of warm sunshine.
In our dressing room I was buckling on my pads when the
bell went and our guest prepared to lead his team out.
He had just reached the door when some gremlin of discord
prompted me to make an artless observation.

"You know, Brian," I said, "I've never made a pair."
His reply was but poor return for our hospitality. He
spat on his hands and he said "RIGHT."

What I had said was true, for although I had as rich
and varied a collection of noughts and nought not outs and
vice versa as any current player, I had never actually
"bagged 'em." My uneasy reflections that perhaps I had
chosen the wrong moment to say so were cut short by the
fall of the ninth wicket. Descending to the turf, I was
surprised to find that Bowes was still present and that it
was his opposite number who had been ousted.

On this occasion I could see by the smiling faces about

me that I was more than ever welcome. The proceedings were formally opened by my old friend Wilfred Barber, who bade me an almost effusively genial " Good morning."

" Ever made pair, Mr. Peebles? " he asked.

" No," I replied, suspiciously.

" My, my," he said, nodding his head approvingly. " You have got a loovely morning for it."

At the wicket I was greeted by another old friend, " Ticker " Mitchell.

" Hast ever made pair? " he enquired.

This time I was ready.

" No," I answered with a fine confidence. "And I fear I am going to disappoint you now."

" You've got a grand chance," he said.

The battle was then joined. The first ball from yet another erstwhile friend, Frank Smailes, was of hissing pace and came sharply down the hill to rap my pads with a resounding thump. The shout that greeted this feat was more in the nature of an explosion than an appeal. It was apparent that not only had every man on the field filled his lungs to capacity as a precautionary measure but that the large Yorkshire contingent in front of the tavern had entered into the spirit of the thing and added a deafening beery blast to the general din. When the reverberations died away the still small voice of the umpire was heard. It said, " Not aht."

Though I say so as shouldn't, I met the next ball with a fine stroke, a push to extra cover—easy one, maybe two. As I cantered smugly up the pitch I couldn't refrain from looking round the crestfallen fielders with a superior smile. This luxurious gesture proved not only premature, but nigh fatal, for it was not until I was near the far end that I looked round for my partner. When I spotted him I came to an abrupt and grinding standstill. He was surveying the scene with approval, even enthusiasm, but from a comfortably motionless position well behind his own crease.

My frenzied summons he heard with an evil grin and after some further unsuccessful entreaty I realised that I was the victim of a sinister plot. There was nothing for it but precipitate and undignified flight. I arrived home at full throttle, just as Arthur Wood knocked all three stumps out of the ground, and this time the home supporters seemed to join in the appeal as well. The square leg umpire was equally impervious to popular clamour and brushed this petition majestically aside.

Order was restored, the stumps re-erected and the struggle resumed—Peebles v. Yorkshire with one given man—also Yorkshire. The ball came flashing down and I plied the same stroke again, now with the vigour of desperation. This time there was the faintest tremor of bat against ball or, more accurately, ball against bat, accompanied by a musical "ping." A great shivering sigh as of twelve simultaneously departing spirits rose eerily about me, and when I turned there she was, the beauty, high above second slip's head and racing to the screen.

Ticker Mitchell summed up the feelings of those immediately present with a few quiet regretful words, spoken from the gully.

"Eeh, Mr. Peebles," he said. "Tha's spoilt bludy morning."

The Bowler

The Man
The Ball
High Wide and Then Some

The Bowler

The ball no question makes of Ayes or Noes.
But left or right as strikes the player goes.
But he that tossed it down into the field
He knows about it all. He knows, he knows!

OMAR KHAYYAM.

CHAPTER SIX

The Man

WHEN A THIRD BATSMAN WAS KNIGHTED within the space of ten years that sage, wit and philosopher Arthur Mailey shook his head and said, " The last bowler they knighted was Sir Francis Drake." Unless Fred Trueman or one of his fellow trundlers turns his energies to some other aspect of public life he may well remain so.

Although the bowler on the whole receives less recognition than the batsman, people are kind enough to say of him that it is he who wins matches. But this, like many other facile pronouncements, is, of course, only partly true, for it is a team which wins any match. It is perhaps completely true to say that, without bowlers of the requisite calibre, it is impossible to win matches however powerful the batting and infallible the fielding, when the element of time is also a factor. Which is, admittedly, a very guarded statement.

The initiative lies with the bowler and what use he makes of it depends on his ability, the conditions in which he is required to perform, and the strength of the batsman opposed to him. Within this broad framework there is much subtlety of psychology, craft and courage which has a profound bearing on the course of the proceedings. There is also in some circumstances a very large degree of physical courage, at least as far as the batsman is concerned.

The bowler has a rather wider choice of method than the batsman in that he can ally himself to one of several distinct types, even if in some cases the adherent hardly lives up to the title. He can be fast or slow, he can spin or swerve, or he can be confined to one of the more precise divisions of those categories. The choice, as a rule, is easy enough ; it is the execution which presents the greater difficulty.

Just as the urgent desire of the normal boy is to hit the ball clean out of sight, so it is to hurl the ball as fast as he can. In days gone by, when West Indies cricket was less efficient but rather more carefree, its attraction lay largely in its youthful effervescence. The batsman slung the bat and the bowlers bounded on springs. They loved to bowl fast and there is a touching simplicity in the device employed by George Challenor to keep his two fast bowlers, John and Francis, at full blast. He merely went to one end and told its occupant that compared to his colleague he was slow-medium, and then went to the other and repeated this harmless exaggeration. The result was electric and, at any time of day, the rivals would thrash themselves into renewed efforts with wrathful cries of " Gimme dat ball."

Everyone should start off as a fast bowler if only to get it out of his system, but he will at the same time, in all probability, acquire the best action of which he is capable. This is a capital foundation on which to build, wherever taste may later lead.

From personal experience I would advise every bowler to delay the final choice of weapons until the latest possible point in his career. So very often those who have concentrated on one particular theme from early youth seem to have lost their promise or missed their true metier. Especially in the field of spin bowling one can recall so many boys who had every promise in adolescence and steadily declined thereafter. Conversely, there are many instances of bowlers who adopted their final form at a mature age and made the highest class. Walter Robins and Freddie Brown were fast medium bowlers in their school days and did not blossom forth as leg-break bowlers until their arrival in University cricket. " Hopper " Read failed to get into the Winchester side but played for England when there was much competition amongst fast bowlers. Johnny Clay and Tom Goddard made little stir in their

fast bowling days but turned into rare off-spinners.
" Chuck " Fleetwood-Smith is said to have been compelled
to switch from fast right hand to left hand googly owing
to an injury.

Many people will, no doubt, be able to cite cases, in
contradiction of those I have listed, of bowlers who have
been consistent and progressive from start to finish, but my
advice to every young bowler is to be catholic in ideas and
experimental in practice.

It is manifestly a very complex subject for there is
present to some extent the question of span. The practice
of any subtle or strenuous activity makes demands on the
physique which in time wears out the mechanism. As far
as bowling is concerned, it seems that the immature are
much more susceptible to this wear and tear and that this
is specially true in the case of leg-break bowlers with the
complicated rotation of the joints. It is notable that all
high-class leg-break bowlers, who have lasted for any
considerable time, have only extended themselves when
fully mature—at least in modern times. Freeman, O'Reilly
and Grimmett were all of ripe years before being called
upon to bowl a heavy season and all lasted well. In the
same period the majority of English leg-spinners were
pushed too early and most suffered from staleness or injury.

It is advisable, therefore, that the schoolboy with ambi-
tion to bowl leg-breaks or googlies for his county or country
should approach the matter with great caution and, having
learnt the mysteries of his craft, employ them but occasionally, as a variation to some less exacting theme.

While believing that the schoolboy leg-spinners should
apply it sparingly, I recognise that the technique should
be learnt at a young age even if it is, so to speak, to be
kept in cold storage. Here there is one sound principle.
Learn to spin first and, having achieved that, turn to
control and thereafter refinements of flight and variations
of pace. My reasons for putting these processes in that particular order are, first, that it is quite a tricky matter to
apply spin to a cricket ball and, in the first stages, will

be a full-time occupation in itself. The second is that the difference between spinning and propelling a ball twenty yards, as against merely propelling it, is so profound that the learner has almost to start all over again. The action and rhythm acquired in learning to bowl straight are, of course, of much value when the time comes to combine spin and control. The foregoing remarks apply principally to leg-break bowling, but are also true to some extent of off-breaks. In the latter case, however, the difference between the technique of the spun and unspun ball is less pronounced.

The manipulation of the seam is very much more simple, if the results are less certain or positive. In this case it is a matter of gripping the ball so that the seam is placed in the desired direction, and only a very slight manipulation of the hand is necessary. In this case the transition from straight up and down to "seamer" is comparatively small and control of length and direction are alike.

There is one important fact I have learned in years of observation and practice, and it is that, if the bowler is of average intelligence, he is the best judge of how his craft should be applied once it is learned. By this I certainly do not mean that anyone should shut his ears to all advice or his eyes to all demonstration. On the contrary, as with any other student, the bowler should actively seek guidance, but he should regard it as such, and having weighed and tested it, must himself decide what is to be pursued and what is to be discarded.

It is an important point, for in my experience I have seen many good prospects disconcerted and eventually ruined by dogmatic orders to bowl faster or slower or spin more or less. Only the bowler himself knows what feels comfortable and right and so engenders that confidence which is essential to successful attack. In 1929 I bowled the opposite end to Walter Robins and have no hesitation in saying he was the most dangerous leg-break bowler in England, and maybe in the world. He bowled his spinners

at a very sharp pace with a long full swing and the ball
seaming lost no pace from the manipulation of his fingers.
He made no attempt to flight the ball, beyond its tendency
to dip from his tremendous spin. At times he was in-
accurate, a fault which would have diminished, but at all
times he was highly dangerous. He made but one major
mistake. He listened to the pundits who, never having
bowled a " tweaker " in their lives, insisted that he should
flight the ball. His experiments in this direction were only
partially successful, and robbed the general performance
of its extraordinary snap and verve. The result was that
although Walter remained a fine bowler for some years
afterwards he never, to my mind, realised his full greatness
nor again reached his early power of destruction.

In my own case I never spun the leg-break very much
but could roll it enough for my purpose, and at least I
could drop it with some accuracy. My life was much
plagued by wellwishers who begged me to spin, saying that
otherwise I would never make a bowler. Whether my
efforts to do so bust my shoulder or whether this event
would have occurred in any case I do not know, but at any
rate it more or less decided the matter.

One time I got chatting with Bill O'Reilly on this theme
and he told me a tale with a profound moral. When he
arrived on the Sydney Cricket Ground and showed his
paces he did not altogether impress the pundits. " Son,"
said they, " you'll never be a bowler until you *spin* your
leg-break." " In that case," replied the forthright Bill, " I
won't be a ruddy bowler."

There are in fact several morals to be drawn from that
tale, and one is that a top-class roller is a darn sight better
proposition than a moderate spinner.

O'Reilly was the best spin bowler of recent times, left
or right hand, off- or leg-break. As implied, he did not
spin the leg-break a great deal, but enough to turn it now
and again. The googly he delivered with a real tweak of
the fingers and his accuracy was unfailing, his pace lively
for his type. Grimmett was a perfect foil and the craftiest

and most consistent of all slow leg-break bowlers. What the pair would have accomplished on some of the Test Match wickets of the 1956 or 1957 series is hard to imagine, but I would wager that not many sides would have topped the hundred on a third or fourth innings.

On this theme many wonder why there is such a dearth of leg-break bowlers at present. It is, of course, a question of some complexity with many factors contributing to the complete answer. One factor is that on these spinners' pitches there is no real call for a leg-breaker where a left-hander or off-spinner can accomplish the same task more economically. This form of attack has been brought to a great art in this country, and England have never had a spinning combination to better Laker and Lock supported by their superb close field. They are ideal for the conditions to which they have been born and bred, but fortunate in their timing for, without belittlement, their methods could hardly have been so successful in the conditions of the previous generation. There were, of course, just as many wet wickets in England twenty or thirty years ago, but I speak of firm, beautifully prepared English Test Match pitches and, albeit without personal experience, of the shirt-fronts of Australia. On these it was only very late in the proceedings that the off-spinner or orthodox left-hander could make the ball deviate. Even the great Hedley Verity, a good bowler of his type on hard wickets, had to wait his opportunity and content himself with exercising his accuracy and resource to keeping the batsman quiet until the rain came. In pre-war days the Oval, now so frequently the spinner's garden of verse, was particularly unkind to off-spinners and left-handers who, if a captain had other resources to hand, were frequently omitted. Douglas Jardine has even voiced the startling but tenable theory that had Laker and Lock served their apprenticeship at the Oval 'tween wars their talents might never have been appreciated, nor been afforded the opportunity to develop.

The truth of the matter is that the left-hander and off-spinner are essentially designed for damaged or imperfect wickets, but the leg-breaker of class can hold his own to a greater extent than any but the superlative quick medium of the Tate or Bedser type on fast plumb pitches. Unless the present trend of ground preparation in this country is radically altered it is difficult to see why anyone should risk the greater complications of spinning the ball from the back of his hand when he can be perfectly effective by means of a much simpler process. Abroad matters are somewhat different and, as regards Australia, I am inclined to prophesy a revival of leg-break bowling for the following reasons. Australia have lost the last two series to England because of England's superior bowling in both instances. On the lively Australian wickets Tyson and Statham were a fiercer and better-lasting combination than Miller and Lindwall. In England there was no answer to Laker and Lock when the dust rose or the rain fell.

Now there is no doubt that the English batting, although uncertain at times, is sounder than the Australian when the ball turns or moves. With these matters before one it would be a safe bet that, if the next series was to be played in conditions similar to either of the last two, England, with her present resources, would once again succeed.

But supposing the next series was to be played on perfect hard fast pitches, the outcome is very much less certain. In such conditions the inherent weaknesses of the Australian batting disappear and it flows in a great tide, as it did in the West Indies. Laker and Lock are then shorn of their weapons and the splendid battery of fast bowlers look much less menacing. The Australians are not only relatively a better batting side on true fast pitches but also a much more effective bowling side, with their spearhead formed by the leg-spin of Benaud. Thus if I were a dictator of Australian cricket I should scrape the river beds for a substitute for Bulli or Merry Creek soil and make every effort to restore Australian wickets to their old time pace and consistency. I would then scour the countryside for any embryonic Grimmetts, Maileys and and O'Reillys. I firmly believe that in so doing I would be performing an inestimable service in the best interests of the game.

In passing I referred to a quick medium bowler of superlative quality, and the present age has produced a very good example in Alec Bedser. There have been three of this category who, in this century, have stood out from a host of very good performers—Barnes, Tate and Bedser. Although all are bracketed for pace they have differed somewhat in method. Barnes, the greatest, was a finger-spinner, Tate was purely a seamer and swerver, but Bedser, in addition to using the seam, can apply sufficient " cut " to break the ball appreciably from the leg as soon as the wicket provides a little bite. It is notable that the most dangerous ball in all these cases is or was the ball going away from the bat.

If their methods were different, they had all the other attributes in common, life, control, action, and in the case of the two B's a great measure of craft and thought. Maurice Tate bowled like a child of nature, and I doubt if he ever aimed to do more than bang the ball down like a cannon shot with all the joy and momentum which a beautiful elastic, rolling action could afford him. It was as though he had imparted something of this dynamic joy to the ball itself in the way it dipped and bounded from the pitch. Not being an introspective performer, he was for quite a time unaware of his tremendous natural gifts and was prepared to jog along as a moderate off-spinner with an occasional fast ball. Some say it was Ernest Tyldesley and some Robert Relf who recognised the true properties of this quicker one and advised Maurice to abandon all else. To one, or both, cricket owes a great deal.

Barnes arrived by the opposite course from starting as a genuine fast bowler but, characteristically, determined this course by his own calculations. An immense volume has been written on the subject of Barnes and his technique so, having contributed my share in the past, I will not repeat myself. The reader, however, may well ask on what authority I dilate on this subject, never having played with

Barnes and only seeing him bowl when 67 years old in
umpire's coat and homberg hat. Part of the answer is that
the last-mentioned demonstration was extremely impressive and the second is that, being immensely interested in
the subject, I have studied a vast amount of evidence from
every available quarter. Indeed, those who have borne
witness are in themselves an extremely interesting and
diverse company ranging from Charlie Macartney of
thirty years ago, and Sir Shenton Thomas, one-time
Governor of Malaya, to the most recent and one of the
most vivid, Bernard Hollowood, Editor of *Punch*, who
played for Staffordshire and saw many glorious performances. He also saw a memorable one which bordered on
slap-stick and which Walter Robins still describes with joy
and gusto. Walter was playing for Sir Julien Cahn's team,
a very strong side, against Staffordshire at Stoke, and was
amongst those shot out for less than 80 by the youthful
sixty-year-old Barnes. The position was indeed parlous
when they came to bat again, well behind, and Sir Julien
took desperate counsel of Walter, who recommended one
and all having a bash. To this bold suggestion Sir J.
replied that he had better lead the way, so that Walter
in due course took middle and leg and awaited his first
experience of Barnes with the new ball. It was quite something; in fact, Walter recalls it as one of the most beautiful
overs he has ever seen bowled. The first was the outswinger which just missed the off-stump. The second was
an in-dipper, and the defender pulled his umbilicus
smartly out of the way as it shot over the leg-stump. The
next was a leg-break and, just to keep things symmetrical,
this missed the off-stump again; a yorker, an off-break and
then the last ball of the over, another leg-break. Trying
to smother it the batsman just snicked it and almost before
it arrived in the wicket keeper's gloves all present appealed.
To their astonishment, and that of the striker, the umpire
said " Not out," and Walter lived to fight another day, or
at least another over. Be it said for Sir Julien, who liked
to win, that on seeing his adviser in such a tangle he

laughed until he cried. Meanwhile Walter had come to a powerful decision, and at the start of the next over, abandoning all thought of trying to parry this superb artistry, he rushed down the wicket and let the bat go. In the circumstance it was sheer vandalism, but it worked, and 16 runs came from the face, edges and back of the bat. This was too much for Barnes who, with the temperament inseparable from genius, snatched his sweater and left the battle to lesser fry.

I could also claim as a source of information the great man himself, as I have the pleasure of meeting him quite frequently during the cricket season, when he attends the Test Matches. He is rare company at all times, but, if you are fond of bowling as an art, it is a great matter to slip a cricket ball into his hand and see his eyes light up as his still supple fingers entwine it. When in his 'eighties he bowled the first over of a match arranged for his benefit in Wales. When asked if he would like a new ball he gallantly refused, on the grounds that he didn't want to get the match over too soon.

The most notable thing about Alec Bedser's start was that, according to him, Eric bowled exactly as he did and in his view would have been just as good. However, there were a great number of seam bowlers at the Oval just then so the brothers decided that it would be in their best interests that one of them should cultivate a different style. Eric therefore slowed down and applied himself to off-spinners, which he bowls very well, but the thought of two Bedsers in Alec's hey-day must bring a gleam to the eye of every ex-selector who had cudgelled his brains to find a new ball bowler to fill the other end.

It is an interesting thought that, while Barnes was always adequately, and at times brilliantly supported, Tate and Bedser, being born into lean periods, were frequently lone hands. Tate largely carried the England attack of the mid 'twenties on his back, which may account for the fact that his peak was of comparatively short duration. He was a very, very good bowler for many years, but a superlative

one only from about '22 to '25, and never afterwards did he
quite achieve the ascendancy of the 1924/25 series in Australia, when it is said his slips stood ten yards deeper than
to any accredited fast bowler. It is true to say that, at least
so far as Australian Test Matches were concerned, he was
never given very much to bowl on thereafter. By the time
Larwood had arrived to give him adequate assistance, his
powers were rather on the wane.

Alec Bedser usually found himself in the same un-
enviable position of being on a losing side and its chief,
and sometimes its only hope of getting the opposition out.
Being enormous of heart and frame, he throve on this
barren diet, and his record of 236 wickets for England is
unparalleled and especially remarkable in being achieved
in such a short time. True he has had one or two easier
targets, but, so far as pitches are concerned, he rather
missed the bowler's market of every series since Australia
1954/55.

His departure from Test Match cricket was in some ways
a sad one, but at least he had the consolation that his last
series against Australia was his most glorious. It was
suitably rewarding that after so many years of effort he
was the major instrument in his country's long-delayed
success. 1953 was the last battle between Bedser and
Lindwall, the greatest pace men of their age and, just at
random, one remembers Trent Bridge on a grey, misty day,
when both at their best produced rare spells of seam
bowling. In my mind's eye I still see Graeme Hole trying
to hit Bedser into the pavilion second over and seeing his
off-stump fly out of the ground. I wonder what prompted
this defiant gesture. Perhaps Hole, in his first Test Match
in England, was influenced by W. G.'s oft-repeated maxim,
"Let's be getting at them before they get at us." Anyway, he
chose the wrong man and the wrong ball.

Over a year elapsed before the trip to Australia, but
Alec was still England's greatest hope. At Perth he was
found to have a severe bout of shingles, and he naturally
fretted at the delay and debilitation. At Brisbane he was

scarcely recovered and certainly in nothing like his true form, but the temptation to play him must have been as strong to the selectors as it was to him to agree. In light of after events, it was a disastrous decision. Thereafter I was convinced that the decision to leave him out was correct, but felt it might have been more gracefully conveyed to him. The abrupt cessation of such a career must have been a bitter blow to both brothers, but they sustained it manfully, for, amongst their many splendid qualities, is a rugged commonsense which blows all nonsense aside as a fresh wind disperses a fog.

The bowlers of post-war years have been a very mixed bag, in which the best of their kind have been mixed with a good whack of mediocrity. Australia jumped straight into the lead with Miller and Lindwall, as good a fast bowling combination as any unbiased critic could claim to have seen. To this they could add Bill Johnston, a particularly versatile left-hander, who could make the most of the new ball or bowl long repressive spells. While Bedser fought a lone hand for England no other Dominion produced a bowler of top class until the West Indies sprang Valentine and Ramadhin on a much surprised cricket world in 1950. The shock to English batting, which had been bracing itself for a blast of pace—which failed to materialise—was considerable. Valentine turned out to be an orthodox left-hander, but of the highest class, a shade faster than most of his ilk, with an abundance of spin which he applied with such power that for much of the season his powerful first finger suffered from a split. His action was always a little full fronted, but this was discounted by extreme suppleness. This fault may, however, have accounted for his sudden decline as a Test Match bowler in 1957, when this lissomness was less apparent. At the top of his powers he was the deadliest of post-war left-handers on all wickets, and in the opinion of Don Bradman the best seen in Australia since Bert Ironmonger.

Ramadhin was not only a surprise packet, being completely unknown even in his own country until shortly before the selection of the side, but also a secret weapon in that no opposing batsman could discern his method of spinning the ball. A dark hand and a very quick action helped an extremely subtle manipulation of the fingers to disguise the direction of his spin so completely that first class batsmen were reduced to impotence as soon as the ball began to turn. A baffled Derbyshire batsman most aptly described his brief experience at Ramadhin's hands as " Trying to play boonch of confetti." The little man, very rightly, guarded his secret closely so that when one day he espied the eagle eyes of the brothers Bedser focussed upon him from behind the nets he put the ball in his pocket and ended his practice.

I would surmise that he spins his leg-break as did Sydney Barnes, between first and third fingers with the wrist straight as for the off-break, and in the but momentary glimpse of the dark hand it is almost identical in appearance with his off-break—at least in this country.

In Australia Ramadhin had a rough passage on the hard fast wickets where his spin, especially the leg-break, had less effect. Australian batsmen when faced with a problem are firm believers in attack as the best defence; and attack they did right lustily on the basis that Ramadhin could, on their pitches, be regarded as an off-spinner pure and simple. After a reasonably successful first Test Match the scourge of English batsmen was all but murdered.

Last year Ramadhin started the series with one of the most beautiful spells of flighted spin bowling it has been my good fortune to see, and at the end of the third day had enabled his side to establish a seemingly impregnable position. From then on he was mastered by the English batsmen, by very different methods from those of their Australian counterparts, and this, with the eclipse of Valentine, meant the end of West Indian hopes of defeating England.

To one who watched his rather melancholy progress it appeared that Ramadhin is still a great bowler despite overwork, lack of support and, in many instances, bad management. If he had the lead of the English fast bowlers and support of the superb fielding he would still be a world beater.

Before leaving the subject it is interesting to note that few, if any, of the batsmen opposed to him in this country can tell his spin from his hand to this day. It is said in the stronger light of tropical countries this is an easier task, and that his slips can guess as soon as he starts his run up. Before the tour started I spent half an hour behind a net at Lord's watching him bowl to Frank Worrell. I do not advance the fact that I had just broken my spectacles as an excuse, for I am certain that aided by them I should have been just as mystified. Perhaps the bowler regarded my presence as less menacing than that of the brothers Bedser, or perhaps he had grown less secretive with the years; at any rate, he bowled his full repertoire. To me every ball looked as though it was cut from the leg and I could find no clue as to its identity. It was interesting to note that the batsman was never for a moment in doubt.

All in all Ramadhin, with his unorthodox introduction and unique powers, has been the most original and interesting of the post-war bowlers.

The English spinners, Laker and Lock, are interesting in their ferocious efficiency on turning wickets, but could hardly be described as original in type. The only hint of unorthodoxy has been in Lock's action which has been the subject of much comment from time to time. It has only been condemned officially in one instance when he was twice no-balled in the West Indies, in both cases it being the delivery of his faster ball to which the umpire objected. Even so, it has long been suspect in this country, and perhaps the most edged and subtle protest was lodged by Doug Insole of Essex, whose castle was wrecked most utterly by a lightning blow. Passing the umpire he observed tartly that he knew he was out but merely wondered whether it was bowled out or run out.

Now one may discuss this matter of action quite freely, even personally, for I am convinced that in almost every case the bowler is quite unaware of his own action, its grace or its illegality or otherwise. There is therefore no question of sharp practice or intention of unfair advantage. It is a problem which has been with us over the years, but more frequent in the era since the war. For this there is, I think, an explanation. First perhaps one should examine the problem as a whole.

The law says that the ball shall be bowled, not thrown or jerked, but does not define the precise difference between the legal and forbidden. It is in fact a very difficult matter to define, but everyone with practical experience of the game has a very clear notion of the pronounced difference between bowling and throwing. Broadly speaking, bowling is a question of momentum, generated by a run up, and the most effective way of utilising this momentum is with a straight arm, through the agency of the back and shoulder. It is an important point that this is both the most effective and the legal method of bowling.

A throw is a sudden dynamic burst of energy generated by muscular power which is best utilised by the catapulting effect of bending and straightening the arm, the shoulder, elbow and wrist joints in a snapping co-ordinated movement. Momentum plays but a small part in this whip-like movement. There are, of course, elements common to both movements, but the basic characteristics have a clear effect in practice.

If you want to *bowl* the ball as fast as you can you naturally run some distance before you instinctively feel the most propitious moment has arrived to let fly. If you want to *throw* the ball a great distance you will find two or three steps are quite sufficient wind up for the maximum effort, and any further movement is ineffective, and in all probability a hindrance to the all-important co-ordination. From these facts several points emerge.

The first is that, contrary to popular belief, throwing is no great advantage to the fast bowler who runs twenty yards. I am convinced that Larwood, Lindwall and Tyson, with their fine actions, could bowl the ball faster than they could throw it. It is probable that there are a vast number of people who can throw faster than they can bowl, but pace alone is not all. It is interesting to note that a number of fast bowlers whose actions were suspect ran but a short way.

It must also be taken into account that as in other matters there are an infinite number of gradations between the entirely orthodox bowling action and the genuine throw. It is possible to have a profitable mixture of both, and a slight catapulting of elbow or wrist can be a useful addition to the swing and momentum of the true action. I remember the slow-motion camera catching a famous pre-war fast bowler at an unfortunate moment when bowling his quicker ball. At normal speed there would have been little suspicion, but under this revealing lens the result must have caused any cinema-going umpire to cry out regardless of his fellow one and ninepennies. Before leaving the faster division there is one point of interest. It is much more difficult to keep the seam of a cricket ball in the desired vertical position when throwing, owing to the flicking, cutting action of wrist and elbow. Because of this very few suspect actions make the ball move much in the air or off the pitch.

To my mind the real advantage of throwing or jerking would lie with the slow or medium paced bowler who only runs a few steps and spins from the front of the hand. He can command a wide range of pace without perceptible change of run or action and the cutting action referred to above is ideal for the off-break or left-hander's leg-break. It is very difficult indeed to throw a leg-break, and the only person I know who could ever do so successfully was Bob Wyatt. It is but fair to say of an old friend that he confined this curious art to net practice.

When I said there was an explanation for the fact that there had been several cases of suspicion in post-war days, it is to say that this is predominantly the age of the off-spinners and left-handers. Although the great majority of off-spinners are genuine bowlers it is, as anyone who has

ever bowled an off-break will know, very easy to shorten
the arm in giving the ball the final flip. It is a very short
step from this slight infringement to what I have described
as the catapulting action of a throw. What is more, it is
very easy to achieve this step with no more evil intention
than putting a bit more into the delivery in terms of spin
or pace. It is a matter of degrees, but I feel that it accounts
for Lock's fast ball being at times beyond doubt an illegal
throw and the delivery of his most vicious spinners
occasionally extremely suspicious. Ian Johnson comes
within the same doubt quite frequently, and I recall in
Australia when he appeared at the nets the visiting
Englishmen would jocularly start throwing off-breaks at
the batsman, a jest which was offered and received in all
good nature. The great difficulty is to decide at what point
the balance is outweighed and the delivery errs on the
side of a throw. Many umpires looked at Johnson as at
Lock, but were apparently satisfied.

In Australia I had a very interesting talk with Bert
Ironmonger, whom most batsmen regarded as the best
left-hander of recent years, but whose action was openly
questioned in many quarters. He talked genially and freely
on this point, and here again it was clearly apparent that
he himself was free of any doubt as to the legality of his
own delivery. He said laughingly that he thought a lot
of the talk was propaganda designed to keep him away
from England. The fact remains that he never did come
to England, despite the fact that most judges thought he
would be a tremendous performer on the softer English
turf. Like so many similar actions, his was apparently
unimpeachable from some aspects, and very doubtful when
viewed from other angles. One of the most interesting
judgments was that of Gubby Allen, who saw Ironmonger
for the first time at Melbourne in his hey-day. Having
heard many comments he decided to form his own judgment, which he did from a broadside view, whence he could
find no fault. He then mounted to the members' stand
and had a look fore and after. Here the effect was a bit

different and Allen felt that there was considerable doubt about two balls per over during the first spell. As the day wore on and the bowler tired this proportion rose steeply and towards the end the observer was pretty sceptical of every ball bowled. This I would cite as further evidence that the bowler himself is probably unaware of any irregularity.

As in the case of the batsman, the basic technique of bowling has changed hardly at all in thirty years. There have been no major inventions, such as the googly was, but Ramadhin and Iverson have produced slightly baffling departures from already well established methods. Tactics, on the other hand, have developed considerably, as I have previously outlined briefly in considering their effect on the trends of batsmanship.

The post-war years have at least been eventful and, intermixed with an unavoidable measure of mediocrity in the restoration period, have had their share of true greatness. In Bedser it has seen the fast medium school at its best since Tate. Tyson, at full blast, has bowled as fast as anyone ever has, but Lindwall was the king, perhaps of all time. The so-called Carmody field, consisting of an arc of fielders almost equally distributed on both sides of the wicket keeper, might have been a monstrosity in the hands of a less accomplished performer, but when Lindwall bowled his fast dipping swingers almost to half-volley length the batsman was faced with an unprecedented problem. When the opposite end was conducted by Keith Miller it provided as stiff a test of new ball batsmanship as has yet been devised.

As the Australian fast bowling declined with the passage of time England saw the start of a great era headed by Statham whose success was closely followed by Tyson's tremendous pace in Australia. With Trueman and Loader following on to provide a quartette of the highest quality, England are well placed at the moment. The first two were eclipsed for the latter part of the last two seasons but, given a good fast pitch, both are still capable of a return to their best form.

South Africa are also fortunate in having two splendid fast bowlers, both with the advantage of abnormally high delivery, and a fine stock seamer in the left-handed Goddard. The West Indies are still a doubtful force in this department but, in Gilchrist, they have a genuine fast bowler and a real trier. The other Dominions have no great fast bowler at the moment of writing but boundless enthusiasm for the game which might throw up a winner at any moment.

Since the triumphant reign of Valentine and Ramadhin the destructive spinning attack has been divided between Laker and Lock for England and Tayfield for South Africa. Now Benaud has come right to the fore and looks like putting leg-break bowling back in its rightful place in the sun and possibly even in the rain. But, as I have previously said, the leg-break wants fast good wickets to achieve its true relative value.

And all the bowler asks is his fair relative place in Batter's Castle—which is to say, bang in the middle of it.

CHAPTER SEVEN

The Ball

IN 1938 MIDDLESEX WERE RUNNERS UP IN the County Championship and, up to a point, gave Yorkshire a very good run for their money. One of our most vital matches was against Notts at Trent Bridge and, again up to a point, things went very well for us. On the third afternoon Notts were still ten runs to save the innings defeat when the last man came in. Nothing could have looked more certain.

But the last pair took root and gradually drew level and then slightly ahead. This in itself would not have been so serious, but down the Trent valley there steadily rolled a great black cloud, bulging with thunder and rain. When the batsmen had achieved a lead of about twenty runs the atmosphere was in a double sense electrical, with everyone on the field in the highest state of tension. At last our captain, now desperate, called for the new ball.

At least one man took a level-headed view of the situation. As I tossed the ball to Jim Smith from mid off, he gave it a rub on his sleeve, looked at it thoughtfully and said, " Look what the silly so-and-so's have done now. Cost the club another 13/6."

In the same circumstances today he might well have been affronted, for the cost to the club of the same ball has advanced to 52/6. This is probably the greatest change to which it has been subjected in a couple of hundred years. For the ball, unlike the bat, has remained, with small variations in size, almost constant.

It was originally white and is to this day made of white leather. The beautiful red dye is set with deer suet and, although there are synthetics, nothing else has been found which does the job so efficiently. It is entirely hand made in the better qualities, built up from a cork core with layers of cork quilting, bound with worsted. The finest balls, as used in first class cricket, are beautifully resilient and softer than the cheaper or machine balls, thus kinder to the bat. A real hard knock, such as it may sustain on being hit into a concrete wall or stand, will put it slightly out of shape, but the next contact with the bat will restore it to perfection.

Its seam, so vitally important to the modern bowler, is all hand stitched, and is a beautiful piece of craftsmanship in itself. In days gone by many bowlers sought to improve on nature, so to speak, by raising the seam by means of a subtly applied thumb nail or a convenient florin. This is now "streng verboten," largely as a result of a row at Worcester when Nigel Haig, a very fine seamer, had a wonderful day on a real green wicket. He made no secret of the fact that he did get a bit of extra purchase by this device. However, there were complaints and it was barred. Perhaps he had been a little strenuous, for one eye-witness, admittedly not one to spoil a good story, said that when the ball was tossed to the umpire for inspection, it split his hand open like a circular saw. I do not hesitate to tell this story about my old friend and captain because I cannot see why the bowler cannot make the most of his implement just as the batsman does of his, and to raise the seam has an infinitely better influence on the game than help of the sporting wicket variety.

In this connection I had a most interesting discussion when in Australia with Jack Massie, a great student of such matters. He is a magnificent-looking man, six feet four inches tall, who promised to be the best left-handed Australian bowler of the century. Tragically, he was hit through the left shoulder in the First War and that finished all thought of active cricket. When he started, every bowler who wanted to used resin to aid his grip, but this too was banned, in his opinion to the detriment of the

game as a whole. I have tried a pinch of resin in nets and
there is no doubt that it is a great help to the spinner
and the firm adherence of the fingers to the surface of the
ball not only gives added spin, but a fine confidence that
one's grip won't slip as it so easily can on grassy pitches
where the ball remains shiny the whole innings. Why
should this be considered any less fair than a batsman
having a rubber handle on his bat and any other device
he requires to ensure his grip?

There have, of course, been attempts to aid the bowler
by making the ball to the minimum dimensions permis-
sible by law, and there is no doubt that it has been to some
extent successful. It is an important point. Even at my
time of life when my bowling is confined to modest
occasions and possibly gives the batsman greater pleasure
than it does me (although I doubt it) I can tell immediately
I get the ball in my fingers if it is a tiny fraction above
average size.

Gubby Allen made some experiments with a considerably smaller ball and got Ray Lindwall to try it out in a
net. The results were impressive, for in the hands of an
expert in the use of the seam, the ball did quite a lot in
the air and off the pitch. It would also help the spinner
whose hands are of normal size or on the small side. But
I personally do not think this is the answer to the ills of
bloated scores as in some lands abroad, and I am certain
that loosely knit dusty wickets are a positive evil. Perhaps
anyone who has read my previous views on this subject
will bear with me, if I once more plunge into a subject
upon which I have been giving forth for donkey's years.

Let us start at the beginning. Cricket, at its best, is to
many people the greatest game in the world. Admittedly
not everyone is agreed on what is cricket at its best. To
some it means village cricket with the ball being hit out of
sight one moment and overwhelmingly triumphant the
next, a state of affairs due much more to caprices of nature
than to the relative skill of the performers. To some it
means the murderous skill of Bradman on a perfect pitch,

a dazzling series of strokes bringing its toll of runs from every ball bowled. To some, Jim Laker taking nineteen wickets in a match, each batsman providing a few minutes of struggling but certain sacrifice. The sum total of which goes to make for that much vaunted "Glorious uncertainty."

To my way of thinking any uncertainty is, so far from being glorious, a very undesirable element in a game as good as cricket. Cricket at its best to me is the contest between batsman and bowler of equal skill on equal terms. In practice, given equal terms the contest will only lie between contestants of equal skill, at least for any length of time, for the weaker party will speedily, and rightly, be eliminated. But on the over prepared and doped wicket the moderate batsman, given patience and determination, can defy Lindwall, Laker or Bedser for long and dreary periods. On the crumbling, dusting pitch the least accomplished spinner can baffle May or Weekes through no merit beyond the erratic behaviour of the ball if he can drop it with reasonable accuracy. As a contest of skill both cases approximate to a tennis match between Hoad and a modest club player on a court of which one side of the net is dirt track and the other centre court standard.

There is only one type of cricket pitch which gives a consistently fair opportunity to both parties and that is matting. It does so because it is entirely true, both to batsman and to bowler, if properly prepared. It is an entirely artificial surface and as such can be designed to fairly fine margins. Given the right foundation, as the typical Dutch or original South African gravel, it is fast, true and safe. The ball will always turn enough to give the bowler incentive and will bounce with unfailing consistency, so that the batsman can readily profit from his rival's mistakes. Hence the game is always alive, for the bowler has the will to attack and the batsman has the confidence to counter attack.

Now I am not advocating the wholesale tillage of Lord's or Old Trafford and the laying down of gravel bedded matting pitches. In the first place, there are drawbacks to matting wickets, quite apart from sentimental considerations. Whatever the subsoil, the bounce is inclined to be steep enough to beat the present height of the wicket from the good length. The bounce being steep and consistent, the slow bowler is at a discount as he can be ruthlessly dealt with by the flat bat. The ball roughs up very much more quickly so that the seam bowler, in modern times a very potent performer, has only a fleeting period before becoming a stop gap until the arrival of the next new ball. In fact, the main force of the attack is confined to the spinner or cutter of brisk pace.

The problem is to translate the virtues of the mat to turf while retaining all the beauties of grass. If this can be achieved cricket will be at all times the greatest game of all to play and the most entertaining to watch. It is surely worth while making the experiment and the effort to match the best of both worlds. The answer to my mind is not beyond attainment and in essence is comparatively simple.

The one thing the enthusiastic groundsman should want to make, and should be able to make in this country, is the perfect strip of turf, solid and unvarying from end to end. Indeed, in days of modern agricultural research it is surely not too much to ask that he could give to this strip the added quality of pace, in terms of cricket, although all attempts in recent years seem to have been unavailing unless allied to a fiery quality, which again defeats the object of balance between batsman and bowler. Given a completely reliable surface from which the ball will bounce consistently and with some degree of life half the problem is solved, but still the bias lies in favour of the batsman. The compensatory factor lies in the hands of the cricket ball maker.

If he could devise a ball which would turn a shade on a really plumb wicket the balance would be achieved and there would be little dull cricket. The bowler would attack directly and the batsman, being attacked, would perforce have to look alive. Soft or damaged wickets would take care

74

of themselves but, if one was assured of really good cricket on plumb pitches there would be a good argument for covering cricket grounds more extensively, and thus being able to play on many days which are, in present circumstances, inevitably lost.

It is not an easy problem to devise such a ball, especially as it is highly desirable to preserve its present feel and appearance. Stuart Surridge, also an expert in the making and use of the ball, points out that it is very difficult to get any turn between the shiny surfaces of a cricket ball and a hard grass wicket. It would not do to rob the seamer by roughing the ball, as this would be robbing Peter to pay Paul. Would it not have some effect if the weight of the ball could be transferred largely to the periphery? Perhaps we could have a committee of experts examine the question, for I am convinced that the logical place to make adjustment between batsman and bowler is at the common link, which happens to be the ball.

CHAPTER EIGHT

High Wide and Then Some

EVERYONE KNOWS THAT THE SPRING IS A
time of buds and blossoms and beauty and burgeoning love.
The cricketer, of course, knows that these are but trivialities and the real beauty of Spring is that it is a prelude
to his own season.

Indeed, for all I care young man's fancy can dither
hither and thither to its heart's content. I am concerned
with what I perceive to be, through the mists of self pity,
a really poignant figure.

With the coming of Spring, in a thousand English homes
the ageing cricketer is fumbling with the locks of his bag,
his mind a turmoil of vague hope struggling against harsh
reality. At length he stands in a hazy atmosphere of moth
balls, blanco and conflicting emotion, sere as his pants are
yellow.

But even at this pregnant moment there are subtle yet
profound differences of approach. The elderly batsman
is resigned to the fact that the ball now vanishes half way
down the pitch and knows his time is come. The partially
ossified fielder realises that, apart from a small and painful
area between shin and toecap, his obstructive value weighs
entirely in favour of the opposition. Not so the ancient
bowler.

Sometime, when the snow has lain thick on the ground,
his hand has chanced upon a cricket ball, perhaps proudly
surrounded by a silver band. A slight manipulation of the
fingers and in a blinding flash he has discovered a wonderful new grip which will enable him to laugh at the years.
A swing of the arm and, at the trifling cost of the overhead

76

light and a few family photographs, he knows that the
spin of Laker and the venom of Lock lie within his con-
vulsive grasp. This will be it—the annus mirabilis, the
imperial Indian Summer. It is only at the long-awaited
net that he learns once more than the paths of would-be
glory lead but to the slow full toss.

Come what may, let us not be discouraged by the dis-
illusionment of the first practice, for 'twas ever thus. Some
may even recall the first appearance of the Wappenshaw
of the Rev. Maister Abercrombie whose arrow, having
missed the target, " passed over two thassie hooses, and
struck in the neck an auld and honest man." I can sympathise with this far from dead-eyed Divine for, when a
lad, I was present at a very similar mishap.

In this case the principal actor was an equally learned
man, a senior and much respected member of Oxford
University and a goodish fast medium right-hander withal.
However, perhaps because he worked hard, lived well and
delivered from the palm of his hand, his early season efforts
occasionally achieved the most astonishing improbabilities
of length and direction. This failing was most painfully
apparent when we took our first net together in the Parks,
and he delivered his first ball of the new season. He
approached the crease with the thrusting stride of the one-
time sprinter and released the ball with a powerful, belting
sling. It was unfortunate that, for an opening delivery,
it generated an immense muzzle velocity, for it caught the
previous bowler, standing two yards to the south-west, a
leaden thump in the region of the kidneys which caused a
prolonged vacancy in the College side.

The offender, apparently unmoved, offered a rather
casual apology and, having received a few high brittle
words of reassurance from the victim, tried again. The
second attempt made ample amends for the truncated
career of the first, for this time there being (understand-
ably) no obstruction to the fore, the ball sailed majestically
into a tree at the back of the net. An anguished squawk
announced the second casualty, an expectant thrush who

saw her home, and exploded maternal prospects, descend in a confused mass upon the heads of the cowering spectators beneath.

The moral of all this, if any, is to keep going. By the start of the season proper my old friend was comparatively safe, and soon taking a goodly crop of wickets. And for ought I know the Rev. Abercrombie may eventually have hit the " thassie hooses " if not indeed the target. In any case, be heartened by thinking of the multitude of bad balls which have taken good wickets. Did not Bradman dismiss Hammond with a slow full toss, and in a Test Match, at that?

Well, the rain has stopped and I have a simply wonderful new way of holding the leg-break. How old was Wilfred Rhodes when they recalled him to win a Test Match?

The Fielder

The Man.
Where's the Point?

The Fielder

Give me the fieldsman whose eyes never stray from me,
  Eager to clutch me, a roebuck in pace;
Perïsh the unalert, perish the "buttery,"
  Perish the laggard I strip in the race.

                    E. V. Lucas (*The Cricket Ball Sings*).

CHAPTER NINE

The Man

LEARIE CONSTANTINE WAS THE BEST ALL round fielder I have ever seen. He could run, throw, catch, stop and anticipate as well as all the specialists in these various accomplishments put together. His measure is best appreciated by recalling the moment when, at cover, he threw down Jack Hobbs' wicket causing the Master, a yard or so down the pitch, to leap for safety, followed the ball to square leg, whence he threw down the other wicket, nearly despatching Andrew Sandham. All this happened in as long as it takes to say "Yours, Hux-table" or "Cor Lumme."

There have, of course, been those who have excelled in particular positions, as Percy Chapman in the gully. He was probably as good a gully as one can be, but has several modern rivals. Richie Benaud, for instance, is a very remarkable fielder, even by Australian standards. His catch in the Lord's Test Match, to dismiss Colin Cowdrey, himself a splendid gully, was something of a miracle in that no bones were broken, apart from the ability to see the ball at the speed and range involved.

But I am not sure the best catch I have every seen was not by his team-mate, Alan Davidson, to dismiss poor old Len Hutton in a Test Match at Sydney. I say "poor old Len" because he had made thirty and was well set when he made a beautiful glancing shot off Bill Johnston for a certain four to fine leg. But not so. Davidson, at short fine, made about five yards in a shallow dive worthy of the Olympic pool, and caught it right on the floor with his right, or minor hand. Just to add insult to injury he caught the English captain twice in the next match, both absolute blinders.

Until recently the Australians have always been a consistently better fielding team than any other international side. Other sides have had magnificent individual performers, but none had achieved the cohesion of the Aussies, who always gave the impression that fielding was a matter of concentrated attack as against an exercise in passive resistance. Now both South Africa and England have produced this quality and add fifty per cent. to the joy of the game by their brilliant efficiency. The present England side is the best in the field in my time, every department being well filled, including throwing, hitherto always a weakness in this country. Australia have always shone in the deep, what with nice, supple, sun-warmed muscles and baseball training.

Of all the great Australian out-fielders the king is maybe "Nip" Pellew. Even timer, strong as an ox and never known to miss a catch—at least almost never. For when I met him in Adelaide we had a lot of fun putting together the details of a famous " double " he perpetrated in the Lord's Test of 1921. Between us we were able to fill this sombre canvas.

England won the toss and, as usual, got off to a lamentable start. This was largely retrieved by Woolley and Douglas who took the score to 108 when Douglas made a terrible mowing stroke at Ted Macdonald's slow ball and was bowled utterly. Nigel Haig, a newcomer, was next in and when he got to the Long Room the Selection Committee set up a howl of desperation. " Go in and hit 'em, Nigel," they cried. " It doesn't matter what happens."

At the top of the steps Nigel met his defeated and highly disgusted captain. " John," he said. " The Selectors have told me to have a bash. What shall I do? "

The reply was scarcely in the " Captain's hand on his shoulder smote " tradition, but, delivered in thunderous tones and sulphurous terms, it clearly indicated that, so far as his captain was concerned, the in-going striker was free to exercise his own judgment.

Arthur Mailey was the first bowler opposed to him, and after a shrewd glance in his direction turned to mid-off, who happened to be " Nip " Pellew, and said, " Drop back a yard, I think we've got a customer."

First ball, the batsman, as instructed, roared down the pitch and hit the ball like a cannon-shot straight at the button of mid-off's cap. The fielder jumped, got both hands to the ball and threw it smartly on the carpet. There was a good deal of surprise at this, but there was real astonishment when the exact performance was repeated off the next ball. The fielder, who still plays occasionally, said he thought he had jumped too late the first time and too soon the second. He sent his best wishes to the beneficiary and asked me to tell him that it was a service he did not expect to perform for him again.

Fielding is one department where the ordinary performer can, by application, improve his powers immeasurably. " Ticker " Mitchell was the worst fielder on the side when he started for Yorkshire and just about the best in England when he finished. Am I not right in thinking the pundits were pretty uncomplimentary about Jack Hobbs' early efforts in the field? He goes down to cricket history amongst the best of the covers. A younger generation have seen his qualities of economy, anticipation and flat accurate throwing in Cyril Washbrook. The Australians have always been well served in this position but they can't have had any much better than Neil Harvey—not even the fabulous Syd Gregory who was reputed to have caught a swallow in an absent-minded moment, presumably on the part of both bird and fielder.

From the sublime to the wooden spoon, that doubtful award goes by popular accord to the aforesaid Bert Iron-monger, prince of left-hand bowlers, who was a finalist for the same award in batsmanship. Mid-on was his chosen position. Occasionally a flippant colleague would place himself there before the arrival of the rightful occupant, who would station himself beside the intruder and, aided by a good rock-like fourteen stone, elbow and nudge him out of the nest. When he caught Larwood, who had got within two of his hundred, the batsman was regarded as a victim of an unforeseen phenomenon and the unluckiest of the match.

Good fielding will do as much to compensate for dull bowling and batting as bad fielding will do to mar fine play. The fielder is a very important man.

CHAPTER TEN

Where's the Point?

AT OXFORD THE OTHER DAY A YOUNG MAN deplored the disappearance of the old-fashioned point.

"At school," he said, " we always had a point."

This plaintive voice moved me profoundly, for at school *we* always had a point. Indeed my finest hour at the crease was brought to an end for the very reason that the science master, combining applied physics with heavily spun off-breaks, deemed it an essential position. The catcher, and a very uncertain one at that, was the senior classics master, who also upheld this station, but more on the grounds of the traditionalism and bigotry common to his ilk.

Let us not blink at facts. To ask for a point today is to lay oneself wide open to raillery of the " Over or under, Grandpa? " variety. Why? Mid-on, once Tom Tiddler's ground for the clumsy, has become an exciting and glamorous post, and has but to advance a couple of yards to be exalted as forward short-leg. Cover point struts like a peacock, forgetting that, as his name implies, he is a mere auxiliary. Anyway, he has now cast off his poor relation and calls himself " Cover."

Consider the point, or a point, or point in his heyday, as illustrated in the Badminton book of long ago. Slips may crouch snarling about him but he stands upright and dignified, arms slightly extended, palms outward, in the attitude of a henwife shutting up shop, or a man appealing to flighty wife or tax inspector. This air of moral rectitude is not, I regret to say, wholly justified in the light of existing evidence.

For in the days long before Mr. Stephen Potter, point

had unrivalled advantages in the matter of "gamesman-ship." He was just within earshot for the muttered aside ("Can't play spinners"—"Bit out of practice"—"Ooooooh"—"Aaaaaah," etc.). Moreover, he was bang in the batsman's line of vision. The rest of the field could run the whole histrionic gamut and be conveniently ignored, but the slightest curl of point's lip was unignorable. The harassed striker must at all times have been aware of the hostile, snake-like eye searing into his very soul.

Not surprisingly that patron saint of points, W. G., surpassed all others in physical and psychological prowess. Admirers like to recall what might be described as the "optical deflection gambit." This called for a somewhat callow batsman and a ball beating bat and off stump by a good margin. Immediately upon taking the ball the wicket keeper would receive an anxious inquiry, "Where did that one go, Board?" and, alert to the situation, would promptly reply, "Just over the top of the middle, sir,"

Point's orbit frequently seems to have been the cockpit of the cricket field. Has not Sir Pelham recalled how, when a callow schoolboy, he was caught up in the mighty waters of a row between the brothers Grace, at point and first slip respectively. His hard cut to the agile E. M. at point was brilliantly intercepted but not quite held and immediately the voice of reproach, high pitched and perhaps just a shade righteous, rang out: "Ot to have cot it, E.M." The reply was characteristically terse and forceful and in the rising tide of battle Board was appealed to by both con-testants. Support for the bemused striker came from his partner, that spirited Bart., Sir Timothy O'Brien, whose thunderous protests that they were disturbing the batsman cannot have done much to lessen the disturbance. At least it must have comforted the young man to know that he was the small spark which had sparked off this mighty conflagration. It must also have strengthened him for the future.

But, as in other things in life, point was not just a bed of roses from which to jab a thorn into the flesh of an

unoffending batsman with impunity. If point availed
himself of his opportunities of aggravation he did so in the
full realisation that he was open to counter attack. No
stroke is harder to gauge in speed and direction than the
square cut and the crafty banderilla could well lend
adrenalin to a batsman's arm. The crushing verbal retort
is a poor thing compared with the spectacle of a haughty
tormentor suddenly bent double, clasping a (preferably)
lunch-filled tummy, or whirling Dervish-like on his one
remaining serviceable leg.

It had been my intention to make an appeal for the
reinstatement of point as lending dignity to the game. On
reflection I feel it might be unwise to press it in times
when international cricket relations are always inclined to
be delicate.

The Captain

The Man.
A Question of Policy.

The Captain

I am monarch of all I survey,
My right there is none to dispute. (Desirably!)

CHAPTER ELEVEN

The Man

I ONCE PLAYED UNDER THE CAPTAINCY OF Sir Pelham Warner. It was in a club match but Sir Pelham led his side with as much enthusiasm as though it had been a vital Test Match. To bowl under his direction was a splendid experience. No point escaped his notice and the field was meticulously arranged, and adjusted to combat each individual striker. When things went wrong the captain always had a word of encouragement for the bowler, so that the most modest performer felt as important as Sydney Barnes himself. To this day I remember the twinkle in his eye as, having seen everything in order, he would say, " I think you're going to get a wicket this over."

With his love of the game, his knowledge, his keenness and unflagging interest in every detail of the play, he was just about as good a captain as ever called " Heads." In the last few hours of his first class career he produced one of those feats of generalship which spring from observation and intelligence. In *My Cricketing Life* he describes it thus: " Previously to this Hendren had been fielding at short leg, but I saw Fender signal from the balcony of the pavilion to the batsmen to force matters, so I promptly placed Hendren in the long field, as I thought a catch was more likely to go in that direction than to short leg, and I wanted to make a certainty of it, and leave nothing to chance." Sure enough the batsman, Tom Shepherd, was caught there soon afterwards and Middlesex won in a tight finish to become Champions.

Monty Noble has always been regarded as the Clausewitz cum Moltke of the cricket field for, in addition to being a resourceful tactician, he was a stern disciplinarian. Sir Pelham recalls a moment when Warren Bardsley, at third man, was rash enough to exchange a few pleasantries with a friendly spectator. This did not escape the eagle eye of his leader who, having reprimanded him, put him near the wicket, where any conversation would be strictly confined to technicalities. Joe Darling must rank high amongst the Australians, but Warwick Armstrong is very difficult to assess as he was never really extended.

It is said that Napoleon's first query concerning a general was, " Is he lucky? " He would have liked F. S. Jackson, who won all five tosses during his reign in 1905, but might have been a bit dubious about A. C. MacLaren, who was always said to be a pessimistic commander. Indeed, I have heard old timers say he was liable to enter the dressing room clutching his head and saying, " Look what they've given me this time." Or, "Gracious me! Don't tell me you're playing!" which cannot have been very good for morale.

Percy Chapman, with his cherubic appearance and sunny presence, was a great source of good cheer to his side, and the most popular captain with the public of the last thirty or forty years.

His successor, Douglas Jardine, was a very different type. Absolutely fearless, determined and unshakable, one had boundless admiration for him if not always agreeing with his policies. I had the good luck to play with him the first time he led England, against New Zealand at Lord's, and I fear I was not very successful in the first mission he entrusted to me. This was to go in number seven as night watchman. I got myself stumped for nought, a feat which caused the rest of the side great joy and hilarity in which the captain could hardly be expected to join.

His opposite number in Australia was Bill Woodfull, a good sound captain with one of the best qualities of leadership, a complete lack of selfishness. Where things were ugliest Woodfull was sure to be, plying his bat like the blade of the guillotine, a shield for the rest of the side.

When Bradman succeeded he soon proved that he was as able a skipper as he was a player, tough, omniscient and very much alive. He had an X-ray eye for everything to do with his side and the opposition, not least fitness. It was said of one ageing performer that he always changed in the lavatory in case Bradman got a glimpse of the network of bandages and plaster which kept him going. Both Bradman and his first English opponent, G. O. Allen, have continued as great forces in their respective countries in after playing days.

Of Len Hutton it might be said that he was a pioneer in that he was the first professional captain of England, but that in the discharge of his office he was notably conservative. His tactics were sound rather than brilliant, but his policy of giving nothing away and making the enemy fight for every inch, paid dividends in the form of Ashes. He beat quite a captain in Lindsay Hassett whose unfailing wit and good humour must have been a great asset to him on and off the field; they certainly were to people who attend cricket functions and hear a good many speeches. I think it was after a war-time match that a local politician thought it would be a bright idea to get Lindsay to say a few words to the crowd who had collected outside the pub in which they were dining. The reluctant orator peered down on a sea of faces from the balcony and in resonant and deliberate tones said, " Never have I seen so many ugly men." The wincing politician recovered his spirits when Lindsay drew breath and added " Nor so many beautiful women," before bowing himself off to thunderous cheers.

South Africa have had a number of notable captains within my span. Herbie Taylor was undoubtedly one of the world's great batsmen but was not a signally successful leader, although it is but fair to say he struck a somewhat lean time. On his retirement from this post, though not the team, his place was taken by 'Nummy' Deane, for whom I cherish a particularly warm memory. He was a splendid leader, a very courageous batsman and as good a mid-off as I have seen. He was a darn good man to play against. I was nineteen when I made 26 in a Test Match in the most unconscionable time, which must have been indescribably exasperating to the other side. I have always remembered Nummy's good nature and his christening me "Stonewall Jackson," adding that I was a bloody nuisance. His spirit permeated his team and relations between both sides were always good, even in the keenest moments.

Herbie Wade did a very good job apart from being the first South African captain to win a series in this country. I know the next in line, Alan Melville, rather better, having been up at Oxford with him. Our first meeting was in the Freshers' Match, in which he made a beautiful hundred, although on the wrong side, at least from my point of view. Alan had the advantage of captaining Sussex for several seasons, so knew his English wickets intimately when he led a touring side. The present South African captain is the first Member of Parliament to captain a Test Match side since F. S. Jackson was a member of the House of Commons.

England look as though they will be well served for some years to come, for Peter May, although already a well-established and experienced leader, must have many years before him. He has the great advantage of being the best player on his side, which gives a captain a ready-made authority if he is a man of fibre, as May most certainly is. It requires a great deal of personality to assert oneself in the presence of great and famous players if not oneself a notable performer. In this Brian Sellers, from the word go, proved himself a very remarkable leader. Although a very fine cricketer after a year or two's experience, he was completely unknown when he started, but he immediately commanded respect of friend and foe alike. I would rate him first of the county captains in the pre-war era.

Now Australia seem to have struck a winner in the young but thoughtful Ian Craig. It is impossible to make a first hand judgment of him as a tactician, as one can so far only judge from reports, but he has had a thumping success on the South African tour, especially when one remembers the doubts about his side when it sailed. He has a most agreeable personality and should be a good diplomat and ambassador for his country.

John Goddard has been a very popular captain of the West Indies in this country, but his last tour was hardly a happy one as a tactician. On several occasions his handling of his bowling was almost unaccountable and seldom did there seem to be any plan or policy about the out cricket. He may well now be suffering from depending too heavily and too successfully on Valentine and Ramadhin who, on the 1950 tour, were usually too much for any opposition.

As I write the New Zealanders are arriving in this country under the captaincy of John Reid, who follows a very popular line established by Tom Lowry and sustained by Walter Hadlee, both of whom did much to uphold the reputation of their Dominion, and that ranks as high with the British public as it did with the late Field-Marshal Rommel, who himself would have made a great cricket captain if his birthplace had been slightly different.

To those temperamentally equipped to lead a cricket side there lies in captaincy the greatest joy that Batter's Castle can offer. To attain it calls for many good and strong qualities. The captain must have the ability to subordinate all personal ambitions to the needs of the team, to a greater degree than any other member. It is often necessary to do and say what is generally unpopular and individually unpalatable in the best interests of the whole side, as the captain sees them. At all times, especially bad times, the captain must give a cheerful and resolute example, and at all times, good or bad, he must be a man of decision. But the captain who can unswervingly follow his principles will gain the respect and very likely the affection of his team. His satisfaction in its success will be something unequalled by the elation of any purely personal achievement.

CHAPTER TWELVE

A Question of Policy

MR. DUMBLE WAS SEATED COMFORTABLY on the heavy roller as the member came round the corner of the pavilion. If he had any qualms at being surprised in this attitude of repose he gave no sign. Having acquired several extra stones since his glorious days as England's and Loamshire's fast bowler, he was neither physically nor temperamentally prone to the guilty start.

" Evenin'," he said, affably, waving his pipe in answer to the member's greeting. " Just havin' a look at things. Great mistake to overwork turf at this time o' year."

It occurred to the member that as long as Mr. Dumble was groundsman to Redthorne Cricket Club they should be fairly free from the fashionable accusation of over-prepared pitches. As it hardly seemed tactful to say so at this particular moment, he handed him his evening paper.

"I see they've made your old skipper President of the County," he said.

"Aye," said Mr. Dumble, studying the announcement. " He's a great man, is Mr. Borrington. Though he were a rare green 'un when he coom to us first, straight from a fine public school and the University. You can guess he didn't know nowt, not t'in-swinger from leg-break."

" He must have come on a lot since then," said the member, thinking of the long list of honours and director-ship which an admiring Press had printed in full.

"Aho aye," replied Mr. Dumble. " It were wunnerful the way he coom on when he got in with us chaps. Very keen to learn he was, and though he were a bit younger than meself we were soon close friends. He learns so much

96

about game and all, that when they makes me 'ead pro they makes 'im skipper."

" He was a pretty good one, was he not? " the member asked.

" He were that," allowed the great man. " Though he were a bit full of 'igh falutin' notions and wot he calls strategy. I had to keep him straight most times, but when things came right he always thought he 'ad doon it, and of course I never let on."

Mr. Dumble relit his pipe and chuckled in such a satisfied manner that the fob on his ample paunch bobbled up and down like a dottle of cream on a jelly.

" I mind the time," he said, " when we takes Championship from Bailshire. We're neck and neck all season and when we coom to play them at 'ome everything depends on t'match; whoever wins that wins Championship. Unfortunately at same time theers Test Match and selectors take most of their batters, but all our regular bowlers, bar meself, so we're in a proper tangle.

" When team's announced I'm sitting in saloon bar of local with Mr. Borrington, having an 'arf pint. Mr. Borrington reads through list and works himself into a fine state.

" ' Dick,' he says, slapping t'paper. ' It's plain barefaced robbery, that's wot it is. They've took all our bowlers and left me with a broken-down old cab 'orse, and a couple of schoolboys.'

" ' Maybe you'll get a bowl yourself this match,' I says.

" ' This is no time for silly jokes,' he says, very testy. ' It'll cost us Championship.'

" ' Not if our skipper has one o' them brain waves,' I says, soothin' him. ' It'll coom right.'

" ' That it will,' he says, brightening up a bit. ' It's brains wot wins matches, Dick. You leave it to your old skipper, he'll get you through.'

" He takes a pull at his tankard and sits looking so wise that at first I thinks beer must be a bit orf. I'm just finding out when he gives table such a thoomp that it takes me a couple o' minutes to cough my 'arf pint out of me loongs.

" ' Pull yourself together, Doomble,' he says, 'And listen. Match is already in t'bag."

" I've heard this 'un afore so I just dries me eyes and says nowt.

" ' You know this young Jack Castor who cooms in for Joe Blackburn,' he says. ' I hear he's best thrower in't country.'

" 'Aye,' I says, ' he can throw, and, as a matter of fact, he's next door in't four ale bar.'

" ' Then fetch him in,' says skipper. 'As he's my chosen instrument of victory he'd best be in at start.'

" So I fetches Jack in and he says ' Good evenin' ' very polite and sits down.

" ' Young man,' says skipper, turning to 'im like he was his grandpa about to leave 'im a million quid, ' you're going to win Championship for County.'

" ' Yessir,' says young Jack, very confused. ' Certainly, sir.'

" ' Now, gentlemen,' says skipper, very solemn, ' what is the chief problem what confronts us in this coming Bailshire match? I will tell you,' he says. ' It is Jim Buckle, a bit old for Test Match, but still best player they have got and maybe best in England. Get him out and with four of their regulars out of side there's only their skipper, old " Shellback " Macsnayle, and we can keep him quiet.'

" ' Can our knock-kneed attack get Jim Buckle out? ' he says. ' No. Therefore we must apply strategy. So you, Jack, will throw left-handed or lob underhand right through the match, until they takes one every time the ball is struck to you. But when I gives you the pass-word " Let her go " you whips her in like a bullet. This will likely be early in their second innings and with a bit of luck, Jim Buckle will be about half-way down pitch.'

" Skipper looks so triumphant-like at this that I thinks he'll fall out of 'imself, but Jack is a bit took aback.

" ' Wot will our chaps think about it, sir? ' he says.

" ' Tell 'em you've busted your arm," I says, ' and you'll never throw again.'

" ' That's right,' says skipper. ' But if you breathe a word of wot's been said 'ere we'll saw your bat in two and sell you to Australia as practice bowler.'

" ' Yessir,' says Jack, and off he goes looking as if he'd just been hit on't thumb by 'arold Larwood.

" I sits on talking to skipper and I says to 'im Jim Buckle is one of t'nicest, kindest men wot ever took middle and leg. But old Macsnayle's 'eart of stone has got hardened with ten years as local manager of the ' Straight Bat ' Insurance Company. Couldn't we roon him out instead?

" ' No, Dick,' says skipper. ' We must be above sentiment in this case. Knock away keystone,' he says, ' and down cooms bridge.'

" Well, match goes pretty normal until third day. We wins toss and makes 253 and they makes 327. Second innings we makes 223 so its pretty critical when they start last innings just about mid-day. Jim Buckle, who's made hundred first innings, cooms in first with old Shellback, and soon they've got 30 on't board, going very nice. Every time they 'its ball to Jack Castor at extra they takes one, and Jack lobs ball back very gentle. It's very hard on 'im with crowd jeering and he feels reet silly. Our captain's at short fine leg and he keeps shouting at 'im to keep up pretence, and winking at 'im to keep up his spirits.

" Presently Mr. Macsnayle pushes ball to Jack and says ' Coom on, Jim, always one 'ere.' He starts down pitch and skipper yells ' Let 'er go.'

" Jack picks 'er up and wot with rage and rest he surpasses himself. I hardly sees ball but I sees batsmen in't middle of pitch so I knows everything's going to be fine.

"And it would have been fine if skipper hadn't of forgot to warn wicket keeper. He, poor man, is on his 'eels, expecting another lob. He just sees ball in time to give a yelp of 'orror and spring smartly to one side. But skipper just behind 'im is theer to stop it, which he does with 'is mid-rift. He makes a noise like someone treading on't bulb 'orn, and folds up like a jack knife.

"We roons to help 'im but he looks pretty bad so theer's nowt for it but to cart 'im off. He's had most of the breath knocked out of 'im but what's left is so 'ot that we have to warn him when we're passing Ladies' Stand.

"Dr. Broom, one of our Committee, is in't dressing room and he chases everyone out except meself.

"'He's winded very bad,' he says, when he's had a look. 'But there's nowt broke and he'll be all right. Still, we'd better get 'im off home.'

"So we gets an old shutter and lays 'im on it and covers him with blanket. Meantime, I've doon a bit o' thinkin'.

"You know, Doctor,' I says, 'I think it might be in't best interests of Club if you refused to make any statement for the present.'

He looks at me very sharp.

"'I think I knows my own business best,' he says. Then he looks again.

"'Maybe you are right,' he says.

"So we sends for a couple of strong chaps to carry him out to President's car what's parked behind and starts out. They wants to take 'im out back way but I says stairs are a bit steep so it will be safer round front. To save him any embarrassment from vulgar spectators I pulls blanket over his 'ead and tells 'im to keep quiet. Then as it's a hot day I takes my cap off and walks behind with it in me hand.

"Theer's a terrible hush as we pass by and, wot with people in front getting up to have a look, soon everyone's on their feet and, maybe because of the heat, most follow my example and take their 'ats off too. We gets 'im snug in't car and just before he goes off he pops his 'ead out of blanket, very depressed.

"'That's torn it proper,' he says. 'That ruddy Jim will get another oondred and win match, blast 'im.'

"Well, I goes back on't field where play's been stopped and Jim Buckle cooms up to me.

" ' We sees him carried orf? ' he says, very white. ' Did he—is he really—? "

" I just looks sad at ground.

" ' Let's get on with match,' I says.

" ' I don't feel much like it,' says Jim. ' I think we should stop.'

" ' Jim,' I says, putting my hand on his shoulder. ' Just afore he was took orf he talked of you. He would like you to go on.'

" Jim turns back to crease, wiping 'is eyes, and Mr. Macsnayle cooms to me in a terrible state.

" ' Wot's this about 'is being took orf? ' he says, very agitated. ' He's as strong as an 'orse, dammit.'

" ' Mr. Macsnayle,' I says to 'im, very stern, ' this is no time for such words. Let us get on with game.'

" But I'm baffled to see him so upset and feel sorry I've misjudged him in't past.

" ' Give me the ball,' I says to bowler. ' I'm going on meself.'

" Well, first straight ball hits Jim's middle stump and in cooms their last real hope, a good batter named Sams. He hits first ball to Jack Castor and starts to roon.

" ' Get back, you stupid fool,' yells Mr. Macsnayle, beside 'imself. In his emotion he calls Sams every rogue he can lay his toongue to, and soon neither knows whether its leg stump or t'Oval pavilion. Sams 'its next ball to same place and this time he's too confused to hear Mr. Macsnayle, and he's roon out by length of pitch.

" While he's waiting for t'next batter Mr. Macsnayle's walking round in circles, laffing and cursing and biting bat 'andle. Next over he's out to worst stroke of 'is life and there's an end on't. They make 74, and most of them is byes, as our wicket keeper acts very apprehensive and starts dodgin' out of road of ball.

" When I changes and goes into Bailshire dressing room atmosphere seems very strained. Jim Buckle asks me wot about skipper, and I tells him that he's out of danger and like as not when he hears score he'll make a complete recovery. Wot with everyone opening 'is mouth to say summat that won't coom out, place looks like bowl of goldfish, but old Shellback Macsnayle cooms oop trumps.

" ' I'm delighted to 'ear it, Doomble,' he says. ' Please congratulate him from me.'

" Well, I gets on't bicycle and goes up to skipper's house, where Mrs. Borrington let's me in.

" ' Wounded hero's sitting oop in't bed doing fine,' she says. ' Go straight in.'

" ' Hullo, Dick,' says skipper, as I cooms round door. " What happened. I suppose we lost?'

" ' No, we did not,' I says. ' We woon. But first, how's yourself? '

" ' We woon!' he says. ' Well, I'm fine, just fine, but,' he says, ' I'll carry trade mark of Seam & Co., ball makers, on me tum for rest of me days. Tell us about match.'

" So I tells 'im what happens and how some people seem to misunderstand, and think he must be worse than is the case.

" ' But there's one thing baffles me,' I says, ' and that is why Mr. Macsnayle was so upset at time, and so reet glad to hear you was all right.'

" ' I'm very touched indeed,' says skipper.

" ' Well,' I says, ' either he's had a change of 'eart or we've misjudged him cruel in't past.'

" ' You may be right,' says skipper. ' On t'other hand, it might be summat to do with my first born, in March last.'

" ' 'Ow could that have anything to do with it? ' I says. ' D'ye mean he's that fond of children? '

" ' No, not quite,' says skipper. ' But when young George is born old Shellback writes me a nice letter congratulating me, and saying that as a family man I'll no doubt want to make provision for the future. The enclosed form, he says, will show that as a fit man of 29 for £100 a year the Straight Bat Insurance Company will insure me for

£10,000 payable at my death. It seems so generous that, with the help of Aunt Aggie, I pays the first premium right away.'

" ' He gives 'is tummy a rub.

" ' Well, there you are,' he says. ' I told you your old skipper would get you through.' "

The Umpire

Popular Appeal.

The Umpire

Shall I never storm or swear,
Just because the umpire's fair?

E. B. V. CHRISTIAN.

The author's fingers twitch as he listens to the world's greatest bowler, Sydney Francis Barnes.   In the background, Ronnie Aird.

A sequel to the Jack Hobbs prank.   See Chapter 2.

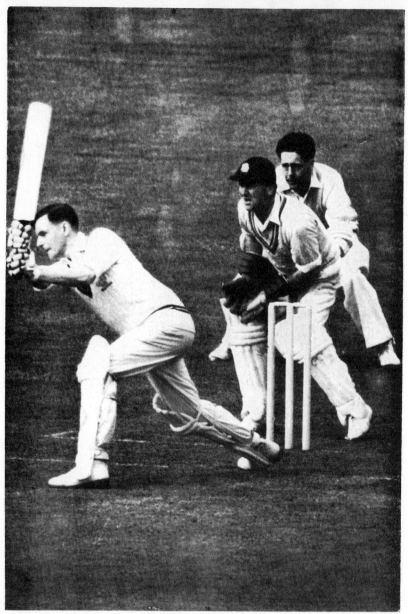

Peter May—power, concentration, balance. An off-driver in the
Hammond tradition.

The best of the bowler's world: Burge loses his middle stump to Statham.

The best of the fielder's world: Benaud's astonishing catch to dismiss Cowdrey at Lord's.

Harvey caught Bailey—another blinder.

Bailey caught Harvey.

The attacking field—the off-spinner in the ascendancy—Laker's leg-side field.

The other end—an attacking field for the ball leaving the bat.

Bradman—sure but lofted for once in a way.

Washbrook—fair and square.

The Hook.

McGlew—too soon.

Graveney—too late?

The fast bowlers on the hunt. Miller bowls to four slips and gully.

Spinners paradise—deadlier to the batsman than strontium 90. The dust rises at Old Trafford.

Elation—Miller sends a souvenir to the spectators on Australia's victory at Lord's.

Tension—May and Washbrook come out to continue their vital stand against Australia 1956.

Gloom and glee—Goddard and Titmus register their side's fortunes in England v. S. Africa Test at Lord's.

Trial and judgment—Laker and Evans appeal successfully against Craig at Manchester Test 1956.

Rare and beautiful—a
square cut as demonstrated
by R. A. McLean of
South Africa.

The pride of
New Zealand—
the left-hander
Bert Sutcliffe.

The two best left-handers of the early post-war days—M. P. Donnelly and
A. R. Morris, both from the Antipodes.

Heave   *Ho*

"Typhoon" in full blast.   A wonderful impression of power and
elasticity.

South African off-spin—Tayfield in action. Note the unusual position of front foot.

Young England—Cowdrey off-drives with a notably open-face bat.

CHAPTER THIRTEEN

Popular Appeal

I ONCE HAD THE TEMERITY TO REMIND AN umpire of his duty. Of course I was very young at the time, and needless to say, the result was not wholly satisfactory from my point of view.

I committed this indiscretion when bowling in a club match to a wicket-keeper whom I had not previously met. A complete lack of understanding between us resulted in an unending flow of byes none of which the umpire, a stout, red-faced man, signalled as such. This irked me quite some so that, when the batsman was presented with yet another four which he had done nothing to earn, I asked the umpire " Was that a hit? "

He went a shade redder and signalled a bye. It was most unfortunate that the next ball was hit far out of the ground. As it disappeared behind a wood in the middle distance the umpire turned to me with an approving air.

" That was," he said.

Which merely goes to show that in addition to having good legs and powers of concentration umpires must be men of uncommon fibre. No wonder in the course of time a fair amount of umpire-lore has grown up.

Some is frankly apocryphal, such as the tale of the obliging stranger who, when asked to fill this high office, said he would be delighted to do so if someone would lend him a whistle. Or the village umpire who firmly discountenanced any appeals directed against the squire. When his patron's middle stump disappeared in a cloud of dust, and a sarcastic bowler said " Well, how was that? " he was equal to the occasion.

" Not out," he said. " But a very near thing."

It must have been a somewhat different type of official who some time ago no-balled a bowler for swearing. One can applaud his sturdy rectitude ; but it is a little difficult to justify his action on legal grounds. Was the penalty inflicted for one great isolated oath or was the umpire satisfied that there was " evidence of system "? Presumably it was the delivery immediately after the offence which was disqualified, for very few bowlers, not even the most arthritic, blaspheme audibly as they run to the crease or actually get rid of the ball. This would put the matter into the category of retrospective legislation which, as we all know, is contrary to the spirit of British justice.

The scene probably ran something like this:

Umpire: No-ball!

Bowler (irascibly): Why? I was behind the line and didn't throw it.

Umpire: You said blankety dash when the one before missed.

Bowler: That's not a no-ball.

Umpire: That is for me to judge.

Bowler: BLANKETY DASH. (Turns and bowls.)

Umpire: No-ball!

So you see, it would be a difficult, if laudable, addition to the present laws.

Judicial occupations naturally breed and enhance character, and when the raw material is the cricket professional the result is rare indeed. Look at some of the names which adorn, or have adorned, the first class list, the King's Bench of umpires—Reeves, Burrows, Bestwick, Skelding, Chester, Dipper, Robinson, Brown (G.), Braund, Dai Davies. What a wealth of wit, knowledge and personality they represent. Lucky indeed is the cricketer who has been able to sit amongst such company and hear their talk of their own and other days.

In this august company Frank Chester achieved a pre-eminence hitherto unknown amongst the fraternity. His sureness of touch and unhurried promptness of decision made for confidence in all taking part. There is no doubt that in later years, when his health was indifferent, this almost miraculous discernment was to some extent diminished. It is no secret that he latterly lost the confidence of the Australians, and relations were slightly strained. He certainly appeared to make a bad mistake in the Leeds match in '53 when, at a most critical moment, Simpson appeared to be run out by a tidy margin but received his absolution.

An Australian appeal is a lusty and wholehearted affair, and not all umpires take kindly to it. Dai Davies, who has succeeded Chester as our leading umpire, has his own views on the subject. One year in the University match he was much shocked by a deafening but unsupported appeal from mid-off for lbw. "Not out," he snapped. Then he turned to the fielder, a beaming, husky blond. "Appealing for lbw from mid-off," he said severely. " It is an Australian you might be!" The offender's grin widened. " I am," he replied.

Perhaps if a ballot was held to elect a patron saint to umpires the greatest vote would go to the late, but immortal, Bill Reeves, with his walrus moustache, piercing black eye, and even more piercing wit. The stories of his doings and sayings are legion. Was it not he who advised a dubious departing batsman to resolve his doubts by having a look in the morrow's paper? Most have heard how he proffered a Middlesex sweater, resplendent with scimitars, to a disgruntled bowler, and was invited to swallow it (roughly speaking) for his pains.

" Wot," said Bill, reproachfully, " swords and all? "

He got at loggerheads with the fiery and equally ready-tongued George Macaulay in one particular match. Having said " Not out " to yet another vociferous appeal, he was heatedly addressed by the appellant.

" What was the matter that time? " the indignant George demanded.

" Too 'igh," replied the adjudicator.

Next over the same scene was re-enacted.

" What in the blue pencil was wrong this time? " asked the bowler in very old-fashioned terms.

" Too low," replied the unmoved Bill.

Umpires too have their perplexities outside the normal interpretation of the rules of the game. I am very fond of the story told me by Bill of a misunderstanding in which he was involved about this time. One morning on a country ground, to which he was a stranger, he was much annoyed by the scorers' persistent failure to acknowledge his signals. When he remonstrated with them at the lunch interval they tersely replied that he naturally couldn't see, as he always signalled with his back to them. Further discussion revealed that what Reeves had taken for the score box was a handsome but wholly unresponsive gentleman's convenience. His impatient gestures must have struck the users as being extremely odd, not to say offensive.

His early days of transition from player to umpire also made good hearing. Somewhere in the West Country he stood, arrayed in umpire's coat for the first time, at square leg where he made a fine but extremely embarrassing catch in the opening over. In another match a little later, seeing the ball strike a pad in front of all three, he emitted a piercing appeal at which the bowler, said to be Wilfred Rhodes, unhesitatingly gave the batsman out.

Probably no type of umpire suffers more in the impartial discharge of his duties than the school professional. Having coached and guided his charges with loving care he is desperately anxious to see them succeed, but so often, by a cruel fate, must be the instrument of their downfall. It is without rancour, therefore, that I recall being given out lbw by one such official in answer to his own confident appeal.

It must be hard for the lately active devotee to school himself to rigid passivity. No keener cricketer than Emmott Robinson ever took the field ; but one always felt that his invincible will to conquer was entirely selfless, and sprang from his passionate love of the game and of his native Yorkshire (in which order I wouldn't know).

I first saw him in a judiciary capacity in a war-time Services match at Bradford. Nobody had much practice and we weren't very good, but the umpire's eyes sparkled as he threw himself into the proceedings with the utmost enthusiasm. Soon he was directing and encouraging an inexperienced bowler with urgent asides to " Pitch it oop a bit " or to " Try leg stoomp." Presently the ball was cut down to third man and gathered by Sergeant Leyland, whose left arm had long been damaged beyond repair. It was easy two in the circumstances, but the batsman, being also young and inexperienced, ran one and then hesitated. The waste of a run was more than Emmott's flesh and blood could stand. Regardless of his cloth, he gave vent to a yelp of agony. " Roon oop," he cried. " You know he can't thraw."

The doyen of umpires is Alec Skelding, great-hearted fast bowler, first class scrapper and a real character who has become something of a legend in his own lifetime. There is a tale or two to be told of him. One dates from 1948 when he had a good-natured altercation with Sid Barnes, the Australian batsman, who voiced doubts as to whether Alec could see at all. Alec wrote him a reassuring letter before the following Test Match, saying that he would be wearing his spectacles in the middle but would leave his dog with the man at the gate.

In the match a dog did stray on to the ground, where-upon Barnes scooped it up and, thrusting the startled beast into Alec's arms, said, " Here's your dog—it must have escaped from the man at the gate."

My favourite Skelding story dates from before his appointment to the umpire's list and, although oft-told, is perhaps worth while putting on record. Upon being demobbed from active service with the county side he was given the job of working the score board at Leicester. Now Alec, a modest man, would readily admit he is no mathe-matician and has no love of figures. The results of his early efforts were occasionally peculiar, and, on this particular day, the information displayed on his board, although fascinating in itself, bore no relation whatsoever to the proceedings on the field.

Dissatisfaction amongst the news-hungry spectators eventually led to a hostile demonstration. Hearing the din, and some very uncomplimentary remarks about his old maths teacher, the cause of the disturbance stuck his head out of the trapdoor and surveyed the confusion of figures, which had grown rather than been planted on the board. As usual, he was master of the situation.

Turning to the nearest and most vociferous demonstrator, he beamed at him in disarming fashion. " Do us a favour, cock," he entreated. " Get us an evening paper, and let's have the right score."

When you sit sadly in the dressing room, unbuckling your pads and explaining to the rest of the side that it pitched outside and would have missed another three, console yourself with the thought that the transgressor belongs to a wonderful fraternity.

Around the Battlements

The Great and Famous.
Birds of a Feather.
How to be a Cricket Writer.
The Great Art of Conversation.
The Traveller—Local.
The Traveller—Abroad.
It's an Ill Wind-up.
Attire and Insignia.
Benefits.
Yorkshire v. Surrey.
Around the Grounds.

Around the Battlements

A pleasing land of drowsyhed 'it was,
Of dreams that wave before the half-shut eye;
And of gay castles in the clouds that pass
For ever flushing round a summer sky.

JAMES THOMSON.

CHAPTER FOURTEEN

The Great and Famous

WITHIN BATTER'S CASTLE, AS I HAVE SAID, the humbler often encounter the great and famous of the world. In this chapter I propose to write of some of the august and celebrated I have struck in my ramblings.

This may sound a somewhat snobbish exercise, but I make no apology. Anyone with a taste for life must enjoy meeting all his fellow men, but there is inevitably something interesting, and something impressive, about the person who has achieved greatness by his own efforts, or fills a great office by right or heredity. To the ordinary citizen it is fascinating to see the impact of fame or notoriety on those who have acquired one or other by accident of looks or measurements, or twist of circumstance or television. The cricketer who travels abroad is likely to meet a fair assortment of all these categories.

The first trip I made abroad was to South Africa about thirty years ago. Immediately after our arrival we met the greatest living man of the country, General Smuts. The occasion was an official lunch of welcome in Capetown. Although my own part in this function was confined to standing to the 'shun and saying " How do you do, sir," I can recall to this day the powerful impression of two peculiarly piercing blue eyes, beneath a very broad brow and an alert, staccato, high-pitched voice. The great success of the day was our captain, Ronny Stanyforth, always a first class speaker, who surpassed himself. The General (as he then was), who had but fleeting knowledge of sportsmen and none of cricketers, was obviously much surprised at this, and, in a very prettily turned reply, said that while he had expected good honest sentiments from a cricketer, he was astonished and delighted to hear real eloquence.

It was some years later that, by a lucky fluke, I met the greatest living man. After dining one evening, Max Aitken and I returned to his father's house, where Lord Beaverbrook had been entertaining Mr. Churchill. On arrival a secretary told Max that his father had been called to attend to some crisis in the *Express,* and had left instructions that he was "to entertain Winston." Max said I might as well come too so we went into the dining room where Mr. Churchill was seated, armed with a glass of brandy and a large cigar. In making the introduction Max mentioned that I was a cricketer, and we all sat down. After a few pleasantries, Mr. Churchill turned to me and said, "You play cricket, young man," to which I replied, "Yes, sir." "Hmm," he said. "So did I." At that he launched forth for twenty minutes on his cricket career which ended at the age of ten with, if I remember rightly, a broken finger. Since that time his interest has been very slight, so he had some difficulty in recalling the terms and implements. However, prompted on the technicalities as he went, the discourse was enthralling, all the more fascinating on account of what the Boer poster described as "difficulty in saying the letter S." "The ball came pasht and hit the little thingsh behind—Eh—Schtumps—yes." There may have been longer, and even more distinguished, cricket careers, but none which for me have had a more absorbing autobiographical record.

Sir Winston's friend and colleague, Mr. R. G. Menzies, is one of the keenest followers of cricket in any part of the globe. He is a big man in every sense of the term, splendid of presence with a fine head and powerful frame. Of his greatness there could be no doubt even to the uninformed stranger, but few of the great can be so genuinely unaffected or gifted with such a flair for, without any loss of dignity, "scrumming in" with ordinary people. He has great humour and a beautiful wit which, allied to

an unexpected gift of mimicry, puts him in the first flight
of raconteurs. A particularly good foil for these qualities
in moments of impromptu debate is Lindsay Hassett,
whose dry swift shafts are just the right stimuli for his
Prime Minister's crisp and immediate repartee.

To talk with Mr. Menzies on cricket is a rare treat, but
perhaps greatest of all is to get him on to the subject of
Sir Winston, for whom he has a profound admiration and
affection. Perhaps he will forgive me for quoting one of
his tales which is revealing of both parties, and to do with
cricket. Mr. Menzies, being in this country when there
was no cricket to watch, did the next best thing, and
arranged a dinner for about a dozen cricketing friends.
He had calculated that his conference would end in good
time to allow him to bathe and change, but he calculated
wrongly. For Sir Winston asked him to wait after the
departure of the other Ministers, and then embarked on
a survey of world affairs. He proceeded on a lofty, soaring
plane which would have been spell-binding at any other
time, but Mr. Menzies, glancing at the clock, had reluc-
tantly to break in. " I am very sorry to interrupt you," he
said, " but at this moment I have a dozen guests waiting
for me at the Savoy."

The Premier was a trifle disgruntled at being brought
down from his lofty plane with a bump, and his brow
darkened.

" This sounds most serious," he said. There was a pause
and suddenly his scowl changed to a twinkle. " You might
be the thirteenth at your own board," he said. Recounting
this, Mr. Menzies merely added, " He never misses."

There was another Anglo-Australian occasion which
gave me a warming glimpse of a contemporary statesman.
The management of the theatre gave a party for Don
Bradman's team and a few other guests during the run
of "Annie Get Your Gun," and, after the performance,
we all supped at a restaurant next door. At supper the
guests of honour were Don Bradman, Lord McGowan and
Mr. Ernest Bevin, as fine and varied a trio as you would

meet in a week's festival cricket. Mr. Bevin was a little late, but, when he appeared at the doorway with his wife, he radiated such a mingled aura of personality and bonhomie that all present, regardless of political creed, gave him a warm and spontaneous hand. When the time came he made a speech, told a number of real good stories, and so obviously enjoyed himself that his audience were captivated, and would have listened all night. However, as he beamed around after some successful sally, Mrs. Bevin addressed him from across the table in a piercing aside, " Now, now, Ernie," she whispered. " You've said quite enough—sit down." At which he did as instructed. Mrs. Bevin must have been, amongst other things, his most successful heckler.

Many politicians are keen cricketers and the Lords and Commons used to play a number of matches. How they fare in these present days of stress I do not know. In days gone by they used to play the M.C.C. and one year they got off to a rough start when four Peers and legislators were out almost without a run being scored. They all fell to a tall, fair young bowler whose spin was too much for them. The non-striker, who had not received a ball from that end, was much impressed and complimented the bowler. " With proper coaching," he said, " you might go a long way." The bowler bowed his acknowledgments.

" Who do you play for? " asked the batsman.

" England," replied the bowler, who happened to be Greville Stevens.

The only match in which I now play with any political flavour takes place annually in Sussex, and the company is very distinguished indeed. Last year the Lord Chancellor opened our innings in rather indifferent light, on a very wet wicket. Running a quick single he slipped and fell flat on his face in the mud, but was up again without taking a count. I brought up the rear with the Postmaster General and, losing my wicket to the First Lord of the Admiralty, a good all-rounder with a puzzling action, felt I had helped to make history. In the same match I took part in one of the swiftest cricket-cum-social events of all time. Seeing a friend, Mike Henderson, with whom I had some business to discuss, arrive at the wicket, I asked him to lunch, hit him on the toe with a dead shooter, appealed, and said " See you tomorrow " all in one breath.

In the same part of the country there is another annual match between a side raised by Hugh Williams against his local village. His team naturally has a strong theatrical element and, as such, is subject to the exigencies of that service. One year the exigencies were so severe that two days before the match rehearsals, television appearances and such-like had reduced our numbers to seven and an S.O.S. went out. There was a good response and, losing the toss on the day, we trooped on to the field. After I had bowled about three rather economical overs, the opposing captain, who had failed to penetrate the ring, remarked that there seemed to be a great many fielders. A count was taken and our selectors were much embarrassed to find they had somewhat over-compensated for the casualties ; there were thirteen men on our side.

The regular actors' side is the Thespids, for which I occasionally used to play under the rule which said, I believe, that teams must have six actors but thereafter could enlist outside help. Owen Nares, Clifford Mollison, Dennis Noble, Sir Gerald du Maurier, Sir Aubrey Smith, and various other well-known actors were keen and active performers in their time. The Taverners now command practically all cricketing stage, film and radio stars, and put together a very good side between them.

One of the most striking and unexpected recruits to cricket from this realm was Paul Robeson, whom I met originally with Mike Shepley, himself a very good school-boy cricketer when at Westminster. I had long been a tremendous admirer of Robeson as a singer and was much gratified on receiving a very warm welcome in his dressing room. This was largely due to the fact that his secretary, "Andy," was a mad keen cricketer who in his schooldays had opened the innings with " Hutch."

Robeson himself at one time lived not far from Lord's
and at first went there as he found it so pleasant of a sunny
morning. Eventually he came to take quite an interest in
the proceedings and took the field himself on one or two
occasions. Being a baseball player, he made a fine cover
point, from which position he threw like a bullet.

It is sad for his admirers to read of his political views,
for he was one of the most interesting people I have ever
met. My education in music is nil, despite a great love
for it, but I remember on one occasion having a great
discussion with him on folk music. I told him the Scots,
especially the Highlanders, were very musical, and he said
he was much interested for he was going to Aberdeen.
When in the North he sang the " Eriskay Love Lilt,"
" Loch Lomond " and several other traditional airs. It was
a measure of his artistry that as high an authority as
Johnny Bannerman later told me that he might, as he sang
then, have been a Highland man himself.

Literature is represented on the cricket field by many a
famous name in the world of writing as, in modern days,
cricket is represented in the world of writing by many a
famous name on the cricket field. In fact, provided that
no too rigorous literary standards were laid down, the
Authors could command the services of a world team for
their annual match against the N.B.L. In practice a
sensible balance is sought, and the majority of "Authors"
are professional writers. Nigel Balchin was good enough
to play for Bucks and so is a pillar of strength. Last year
Edmund Blunden returned from the East to lead the side
with craft and resource, not to say considerable skill.

One year Paul Gallico made his bow on the cricket field
in the Authors v. the N.B.L., albeit on the wrong side.
This was due to the fact that we were over-subscribed when
it was known that he was available. He was not entirely
new to the subject, for some time before we went together
to a Test Match against New Zealand at the Oval when
we were both connected with the *Sunday Dispatch*. It was
an interesting experience to meet the author of the *Snow*

Goose and other such sensitive writings. He was a New York sports and boxing correspondent, though anything but " beefy," as a derogatory reviewer described him the other day. Our outing was a success, for being a games player he took an intelligent view of the play and his impressions were most interesting. Could other Transatlanic celebrities please note? Any Americans I have introduced to cricket, and what with war time there have been plenty, have been keen to know what goes on and fun to instruct, but the famous American is somehow expected to make a crack about cricket, so we have the same sad, well-tried but wobbly little jokes all over again. Even that superb man, Groucho Marx, grimly compelled to be funny, flopped on the subject.

Danny Kaye, on the other hand, came into the Lord's dressing room, charming, grave, polite, and talked golf with Denis Compton.

On the subject of American visitors being compelled to say something, a rather humbler party once turned up at Lord's in the shape of the American Y.M.C.A. As captain of Middlesex I helped Billy Findlay, then secretary, to show them round. The visitors were most appreciative but, being elderly and not interested in cricket, found it as difficult to keep up a flow of polite comments as we did to entertain them. When we got back to the Long Room both sides were obviously exhausted and searching for words. However, as a grand final gesture the secretary indicated the bust of W. G., saying " That's Dr. Grace, the greatest cricketer of all." The visiting leader, a small grey man, strove desperately for just one last good line. " Say," he enquired, " is the Doctor in practice? "

With the war-time invasion cricket gained a number of American adherents, or at least their interest. In London district I used to run an unofficial course for visiting Americans. This consisted of an exposition on the back of the menu at lunch time before going to a Services match. From this I learned one thing of value to all who seek to introduce a stranger to Batter's Castle. See that the novice knows something about what happens before he sets out.

One of these interested parties was Dick Vidmer, who used to be a sports columnist on the *New York Herald Tribune,* and to whom I used to listen enthralled as he told his tales of the world's champion fighters, all of whom he knew intimately. It was with him that I met Bobby Jones, who was his half section in the American Air Force, and one of the most pleasant celebrities I have met, friendly, modest and great company. He astonished me, when we sat down to dine, by asking what a Yorker might be. When he had digested the answer he enquired about a maiden over. At this I asked him how he came to know all these terms. He replied that when in his heyday and winning everything he used to lessen the nervous tension by having breakfast in bed, with the *Times* for his reading. He got very interested in the Test Matches and, although the game was a mystery to him, the figures and terms fascinated him. After fifteen years he remembered most of them and a number of the players' names, though not, I think, my own.

It was with Dick Vidmer that I met Joe Louis. His only connection with cricket was that he was taking part in a sporting exhibition at Earls Court and next door to his dressing room were Denis Compton and the brothers Bedser who were doing a cricket act. I had the honour of introducing these various distinguished parties to each other and Joe was much struck with the manly physique of the brothers. I believe that he later made some tentative suggestions that they might join his camp.

As a sequel I recall that the exhibition was a financial frost and there was some delay in payment of balances by the promoter who, in contrast to his employees, was a very small man. In the midst of a heated dispute Denis, exasperated, made a menacing, if unintended, gesture in his direction, at which the little man shot backwards to his full five foot none with a defiant " Vait till I get my glasses off ! "

Royalty has always patronised cricket as a truly British institution, but only in modern times has it taken such an active, able part. The Duke of Edinburgh is a good off-spinner in addition to being a fine free swinging batsman, and the Queen is said to be a keen follower. Her Majesty's visits to Lord's have always been wonderful occasions and somehow far transcend the ordinary occasion. There is indeed at times something intensely moving about such scenes. I remember standing on the top tier of the pavilion with Tom Killick, an old colleague and rival, as the Queen went forth to greet the South African side. The sun shone as she went in youth and dignity, watched in silent admiration by all, but by some who must have known five reigns, to talk so easily and naturally with the visitors of her own generation. Tom spoke for everyone there. He just said, " It makes you proud."

George the Fifth was not much interested in cricket but he also used to come to Lord's to meet the Dominion teams. Characteristically, when the Empire resounded with the " Body Line " dispute, he felt it his duty to ascertain the facts for himself. Gubby Allen says that he achieved a clearer and more balanced view of the situation than anyone else he met.

The Duke of Windsor, when Prince of Wales, came to the Australian Test Match at the Oval, possibly because it was Jack Hobbs' last appearance for England. When he arrived Duleep and I were alone in the dressing room and rather dejected, having spent two days in the field and fearing we might well be there for another two. The Prince had obviously been hastily briefed for he said to me, " You have just come down from Cambridge, haven't you? " to which I perforce replied, " No, sir. I'm still up at Oxford." There was a slight hiatus and he then said to Duleep, " Of course, you're still up at Oxford? " To which " Smith " replied with some embarrassment, " No, sir. I came down from Cambridge two years ago."

On the whole we felt that our occasion hadn't been an

outstanding success, but we had gained some insight to the trials Royalty must have to bear.

There has always been some affinity between cricket and the Law, but perhaps the greatest gift which that august institution has given to cricket is the eloquence of Lord Birkett, a great lover and follower of the game. A Birkett innings is a thing of great joy—the beautiful delivery, the inspired prose, the impeccable timing and the incomparable wit. Not so long ago I myself had to propose the health of the guests at a cricket dinner, the reply being in the most capable care of Mr. Tommy Trinder. Seeing, not without trepidation, Lord Birkett sitting opposite, I said I had no doubt that the rest of the company shared my heartfelt wish that it was he, not me, who happened to be addressing them. The agile Trinder seized on this, saying that, judging from his recent experience of litigation, I must be one of the most affluent citizens of London, if I could ask Lord Birkett to speak for me. His Lordship smiled a wry smile at this, as well he might when he considered the vast amount of speaking he has done at some expense to himself, and the tremendous pleasure he has freely dispensed.

On really special occasions one may also strike on the same bill Lord Monckton, a very able cricketer who played at Lord's for Harrow. The exchanges between two of such calibre are naturally a magnificent entertainment. At the dinner for the centenary of Old Trafford, Lord Birkett delighted the Lancastrians with a splendid tribute to his colleague, saying that even in the cricket world his name was recorded for all to revere. His audience had been swept to a fine pitch of elation by the grandeur of this address, when he solemnly read out "W. T. Monckton b Fowler o."

As I go to press the newspapers quote Mr. Menzies as saying that if Russia and America played cricket the world would be a better place. Should I return to this subject in the future it would be nice to say I had bowled to Mr. Kruschev at the Lord's Easter Classes.

CHAPTER FIFTEEN

Birds of a Feather

THOUGH ALL ARE SPRUNG FROM THE SAME source the cricket spectator, as a species, is a very variable bird.

Possibly in his highest expression he is to be found in the upper branches of the great migratory at St. John's Wood where, during the season, he sits silent and motionless for long periods on end. His plumage is drably designed to avoid attracting attention and, in recent years, his crest has been truncated and his tail feathers have almost disappeared. Years of breeding have rendered his cry almost inaudible but patient listeners, by straining their ears, may occasionally hear a dulcet " Welplaidser " indicative of the bird's pleasure. If displeased this branch of the species is seldom vocal, but relies on a series of ritualistic signals, which it lodges in the office of the secretary bird.

In other game reservations in the English counties, and more especially overseas, one may find a very different development of the strain. This variety is essentially gregarious, and likes to flock in great numbers on banks and hillsides. Its plumage is unpredictable but its presence is readily recognisable by its cry, which is loud and penetrating. It is somewhat excitable in temperament and not always very discerning, so that it suffers many moments of stress and sharp changes of mood. During these periods it gives forth deafening sounds, extremely alarming to quieter birds which have come to roost in the neighbourhood. Sometimes the cry is hollow and booming, sometimes muffled and liquid, often sawlike and occasionally, in the case of the young birds imitating the old ones, squeaky and very trying. In most instances the cry is the same and goes "Ave-a-gaow," "Gercha" or "Gitabag."

In certain places female birds are plentiful and secluded areas are reserved for them. Here they make a pleasant spectacle with their more brilliant colouring, and there rises from the flock a continuous clucking and buzzing. It is probably on account of this last phenomenon that arrangements are made for their segregation as the male bird, if within earshot, is liable to evince signs of great perturbation in the shape of hissings and snortings accompanied by menacing looks and gestures. If suddenly alarmed or excited the female flock is wont to give out a shrill piercing cry in unison, delivered fortissimo and sostenuto.

A remarkable example of the female has been observed for some years in this country and is known to the cognoscenti as "Yorkshire Annie." So commanding is this bird's aspect and so powerful her song that certain wardens, fearful of the effect of her presence on other birds, have occasionally sought to harry her from their preserves.

There then is today's ornithology lesson. But talk of birds and spectators takes me back to Lord's, where a friend of mine claims to have overheard the following conversation during a rather humid pause in the proceedings.

First Elderly Member: "Extraordinarily badly run, this place, sir. Birds on the wicket."

His companion (with hauteur): "Yes, sir, common birds, too—sparrows."

Aye, and it might well be true, for until the war Lord's boasted quite a number of engagingly eccentric spectators. They would sit around, in the apt words of "Crusoe" Robertson-Glasgow, "asking questions which would never be answered, answering questions which had never been asked."

It was a little further afield at a school match that the Robins family overheard one of last season's prize winners. Nearby was another family headed by Uncle, a man of ample presence and colourful countenance. But the pre-prandial play lagged and soon he nodded off to a profound slumber. It was just before lunch that the batsman suddenly struck a couple of fours and Niece, an ardent supporter of the batting side, cried gleefully, " Now we're forging ahead."

Uncle shot from his slumbers as the old war horse leaps to the trumpet call.

" Eh, what's that," he asked in urgent tones. " Who's four gins ahead? "

The only catch to these gems uttered in august surroundings is that they fall on but a few privileged ears. If the Hillite at Sydney has anything good to say, on the other hand, up to 80,000 people get full and immediate benefit. My own favourite observation, however, emanated from a pundit at the rival centre of Adelaide long ago when Charlie Kelleway made a hundred against Johnny Douglas' side and took over seven hours in doing it.

Well, here he is around the seventh hour when he has reduced friend and foe alike to a despairing silence. But here's a bowling change and a tired and elderly bowler runs up and delivers a very slow straight ball. And here at last is action too! The batsman picks up the bat, he rushes down the pitch. He's going to belt the ball right out of sight. No. At the last moment he restrains himself and stops her dead. The bowler releases another weary half volley and this time—hooray—we're going to see something. The batsman dashes to meet the ball—he's got the bat poised—he's going to—er, no, he's changed his mind again. Heigh-ho. But this time—look out!—he's down the track—he's winding up—goodo—it's a—its' a—aw, dear. As the bowler advances to collect the stationary ball the pundit addresses the batsman on behalf of all present.

" You bloody liar," bawls this disillusioned man.

It was in the later stages of a rather similar innings by Trevor Bailey that a weary spectator disturbed the prevailing silence with a heartfelt cry of " Byley, I bet they was glad when you left England."

And of overseas spectators we wind up where we started. For was there ever a more entrancing company than the West Indies supporters who congregated in the free seats when their team won their first Lord's Test Match. As James Swanton said, the whole block looked as though someone had burst a bag of soot over it. Do you remember when Cyril Washbrook, beaten by a leg cutter from Ramadhin, looked suspiciously at the spot on which it had pitched and gave it a tentative prod? Immediately a vast Robesonic base rolled out of the dark cloud like a 21-gun salute.

" Dat was not de pitch—it was de BOLAH."

On the last West Indies series the most notable spectator was of sturdy home grown variety. He sat next to a friend of mine on the popular side during the Thursday and Friday of the Birmingham Test and was an honest son of toil, gifted with a fine wit, a wide general knowledge and a great love of cricket. My friend was entranced by his company and, when the time came to part on Friday evening, he said how very much he had enjoyed their two days together and much hoped they would meet again on the morrow.

His new friend greeted this address with astonishment and reluctance. "What? " he said. " Me watch cricket on my day off? Not bloody likely."

And when the more advanced school of sculpture is twisting wire into memorials for various unknown citizens what about something to commemorate the unknown genius who originally cried out " Get a bag." How about a wooden bench surmounted by an outsize bag—full of wind?

CHAPTER SIXTEEN

How to be a Cricket Writer

SOME YEARS AGO I HAD THE HONOUR OF introducing the late Charles Fry to my then newly acquired wife. He was dressed in a smock-like shirt of his own design with a neckband of somewhat clerical cut. This was surmounted by a terai, the double-brimmed hat favoured by the Boer farmer and other workers under the equatorial sun, with the resultant effect of a tropical mission of the Greek Orthodox Church.

He greeted her with his customary courtliness, and almost immediately was launched into a dissertation of great technical brillance on the reasons why Hobbs, in playing back, retained the position to score past mid-on. My wife, being at that time completely unversed in the mysteries of the great game, was nigh overwhelmed, but much cheered when, to illustrate his point, he snatched a neighbouring stranger's umbrella, precipitating the owner, who happened to be leaning on it at that moment. The point of his address, if not altogether appreciated by the startled stranger, was that cricket was an art which could not be taught, but must needs be handed down by precept and example.

Whether Fry believed the same of cricket writing, in which he also excelled, I do not know, but I feel that it is an arguable point of view. In any case, having embarked under this ambitious chapter title, I am bound to say that, apart from a few rudimentary rules, obvious to all, I have no idea how in the heck you become a writer on any subject. It will therefore be convenient, nay imperative, in this case to regard cricket writing as art to be handed down by precept and example, and crib what we can from the works of the established. I am sorry if you were in any way misled by the title; but this is the best I can do for you.

First the rudimentary rules. In almost any press box you will want sweaters and woollies in the proportion of two to one to those worn on the field. If you are prosperous enough to own a pair of binoculars keep the strap round your neck fairly short. The press box is a matey, co-operative place and this will mean that, even if you cannot see through your own glasses, they cannot be further away than one neighbour due N., S., E. or W. If your spelling is anything like mine it is advisable to carry a pocket dictionary, as this will do something to diminish the kindly contempt with which telephonists, sub-editors, compositors, etc., must inevitably regard your masterly prose.

So much for the mechanics of your profession. Now a most important aspect—psychology. And this means the study of the Editor, at a distance, and the Sports Editor more intimately. Should they be producing something on the lines of *The Times* it is improbable that they will be looking for "angles," "exclusives" or "revelations." On the other hand, the readers of *The Daily Splash* are unlikely to revere quotations from Horace. Having grasped these principles all that remains is a little guidance on how to word an expense sheet and you are off.

Here then is a simple practical exercise in the various methods of dealing with a day's play, summarised on the Television News as—' The Test Match. England declared their second innings closed at 482 for seven wickets. Hogshead batted all day and was not out at the end, having scored 224."

The first great school for your contemplation is the orthodox and traditionalist. This is a difficult one, for it entails not only a profound knowledge of the game itself but also of its history, manners, customs and traditions, for of these you are the vigilant custodian and protector. Thus:

" Yesterday at Lord's, admittedly in chilly weather, a young batsman went to the wicket wearing a flannel balaclava helmet in the shade of blue appropriate to his university. It is not for an older generation to discourage progress and innovation ; but, in a case where the innovator infringes the rules of decorum and taste, it may be appropriate to draw his attention to the somewhat rigid sartorial code established and enforced by W. T. (Bully) Pockleton in the early 'seventies. One of its less exacting clauses provided that any member of the XI wearing turn-ups on his trousers should be publicly flogged round the outfield with his own braces. Such restriction and penalty may seem totalitarian to modern eyes, but have we not travelled rather too far in the opposite direction?

Despite this distraction it was a fine day's cricket, during which England increased their overnight score to 482 for seven wickets on a wicket which the early dew had rendered a treacherous surface on which to counter Flockerty's skilful manipulation of the seam. Later a slight superficial disintegration gave purchase for Moriarty's diagonally spun leg-breaks. The chief architect etc. . . ."

On the same level, but rather less technical, is the romanticist who sees the game through a cultured and visionary eye. It is seemingly a harrowing experience and its translation has the snag that it calls for a considerable degree of education on the part of both author and reader. Still, if the reader is baffled from time to time so much the better. There is at the present time a great opportunity for a revival of this school.

" Umpire Boggins crouched over the wicket entrusted to his care, his white coat streaming behind him, a toga symbolic of the stern justice it was his to dispense. His face was a mask of pain as he strove to utter the pregnant syllable which would raise the curtain on the last act of this drama, so delicately poised between tragedy and farce. ' Play!' In the oppressive silence there seemed to echo the rattle of some ethereal firing squad, mowing down our faint remaining hope in bloody disorder.

" But between the grim-visaged Flockerty, thundering Valkyrian to the crease, and final annihilation stood two champions so different they might be born of different planets. The buccolic effervescence of Hogshead threw into agonising relief the delicate tracery of Button's weaving wrists, searching vainly midst the perils of the off. The scene was set as surely as Snouton's production of Burkwasser's *Gheistein mit Phunffbach*. To the metaphysician . . .."

Never mind, England still declared, a fact you will have to present rather differently if your appointment is to one of the racier journals. The reader whose eye has fallen on the sports page fresh from " Bigamous Burglar's Dramatic Outburst " will demand some stronger meat. As you will probably be presented to your public as " The World's Greatest Cricket Writer " or " The Man They'd Like to Strangle," the first step is to put yourself in proper perspective in relation to the subject and the reader. A positive rather than objective attitude is called for, so don't just kick off by saying you have been to a press conference:

" Portly, parrot-faced Panton Festonhaugh de Vere Binks, third Baron Brum, President of the M.C.C., was waiting for me at the gate. ' Thank goodness you're here, Blabberty,' he boomed. ' There is real trouble with the Australian captain.' I brushed him impatiently aside and hastened to the ancient ivy-clad dressing room where the trouble was just as I had figured. The gangling, crew-cut cornstalk burst into tears when I told him he was holding the bat the wrong way round and the bulge should be *at the back*. ' But they go better sideways,' he protested. ' Get wise to yourself, Ned,' I advised. ' Take a look ahead—no fielders.'

" As the day went he didn't get a break as the Gloamshire glamour boy, taking my advice about an early night once in a while, slammed his side to a sensational declaration.

" The President left the Committee room to see me into

his sleek crested limousine. ' Nice work, Snip,' he chuckled as we slid through the armorial-bearing gates."

That about covers the field of day-to-day commentary in this country, but in other parts of the world there is a really red-blooded school. The column is the ideal firing platform for this performance as it provides an all-round field, and it should have a subtly challenging title such as "Want Your Teeth Kicked In?—Come On." However, the style is readily applicable to straightforward description:

" Eleven shambling zombies hauled out of their simpering dotage by despairing, ham-handed selector Stiggins tottered on to the field at Lord's yesterday. Their scrawny necks could hardly support the Australian caps they had the cheek to wear. Bradman would have eaten the lot for breakfast and coughed them up again before lunch. They couldn't even get the ageing, decaying Gloamshire beauty queen out—not even before he got the gin and fog of El Paradiso out of his bloodshot eye. You're digging your own grave, Stiggins—go on, get in it before you dig one for Australian cricket."

If you think this is your metier it is a good plan to have a few words with the legal department before introducing this particular style to this rather old-fashioned country.

Finally, a very different cup of tea. It is unlikely that you will be called upon immediately to record these mighty events for posterity, but it is just as well to be prepared. In this case, despite the rather damping prospect of complete anonymity, it is satisfactory to reflect that your words will likely be quoted by generations yet unborn. With this responsibility in view the style must of necessity be more in the White Paper tradition, but with a nice judicial flavour. In recent years the chroniclers have become almost brisk, but for my taste, as for millions of other fireside readers, the older school. Here we find a distinctly Teutonic flavour in that the main verb comes at the end of a lengthy and meaty sentence, so that the reader has all the delight of his first birthday cake, when he left the icing until the very last:

"Occupying the crease for a period of four and three-quarter hours, driving powerfully and excelling in the cut, although in early difficulty with Flockerty's express deliveries and missed at 92 and 151 in attempting to force the pace, despite a tendency to hit against the spin, Hogshead was undefeated when England declared their innings closed at half past four o'clock. During this prolonged episode there were times when the tactics of the Australian captain, apparently troubled by some indecision regarding his present method of gripping the bat were, not to put too fine a point upon it, adjacent to the confines of lunacy."

P.S.—An eminent journalist who was kind enough to help me in correcting the proofs of this book points out that I have omitted one school of journalism which he jocularly calls "The Weekly Woffle." He has rectified this omission by sending me a sample devoted to a slightly different subject; one which he says gives this type of writer full scope. Personally, I do not recognise the school, but can appreciate that it is thoughtful, knowledgeable, readable, prescient and reliable. I therefore print this extract as being a rewarding study for the ambitious young journalist.

"When it comes to picking the bowlers for the M.C.C. tour of Australia the selectors, for all the wisdom and experience of Mr. Allen and his subordinates, will be up against a task which your correspondent for one, with his canny Scots upbringing and—dare I say—having known, albeit in a humbler role as sometime Muddlesex captain, the divers factors, unappreciated by the uninitiated but ever-present in the minds of those whose job is to shoulder the responsibility, certainly does not envy them.

"If I may venture to say a word, it is that the choice of the right men is all-important. In the first place one must gauge the correct number—for it is as embarrassing to have too many quickies and tweakers aching to turn their arms as it is to have to take the field without a balanced attack equipped for all wickets and to suit all the range of conditions that the side may reasonably expect to encounter. Then comes the question of variety, and here is the nub. For though it was the quick who were the basis of success last time wickets are unpredictable things, and it may well be that the curators (to use the idiom of Down-Under), with the best will in the world, will find themselves nurturing, in the swiftly-changing climate that is apt to be encountered in the sub-continent, a very different sort of surface such as will draw the teeth of Statham, Tyson, Trueman, Bailey, and (if he should be chosen, and that is a matter which cannot be decided without due thought and consideration nearer the time) Loader, and may leave our alert and thoughtful captain sighing for a more crafty form of attack, or perhaps for a stock trundler of the type of Alec Bedser, who though possibly just past his peak . . . I will consider these in due course. . . ."

So now you know.

CHAPTER SEVENTEEN

The Great Art of Conversation

NO DOUBT ANY UNNECESSARY TALKING ON the cricket field is very bad form and to be greatly deplored and discouraged. On the other hand, cricketers are a gregarious and madly loquacious sect so that, however much the disciplinarian may deplore the chit chat about him, he will find it uphill work discouraging it.

In a fairly long and fairly wide experience of the game I have encountered as many different types of conversationalist on the cricket field as one might meet in a week's drinking bout with representatives of all the United Nations. There have been the genial and ingenuous, the shrill and carping, the foolishly optimistic and the habitually gloomy, the brave and truculent and the shy and apprehensive. There have been wofflers, stutterers, whistling dentures, profaners, sibilant orientals, booming senior officers and bronchial veterans, all contributing to the hum of human intercourse which rises unceasingly under the never setting sun of the cricket world.

The first type which springs to mind is the warm, kindly individual whose good nature is such that, to remain silent in the presence of a fellow creature, seems to be churlish and even hostile. He is usually to be found in the region of mid-on as he lacks the predatory nature to be a good slip or short leg. He is probably happier between overs than when the game is actually in progress, as he is then untrammelled by black looks from the bowler, and the tart hints from his captain as to his being quite ready. The beau ideal of this type must always be Maurice Tate. True, the elaborately confidential delivery was liable to overawe the uninitiated and mislead the onlooker into the belief that he was propounding something of a dire and fearsome nature. This was certainly not so, as his remarks were ever of a highly conversational nature, such as two gentlemen might exchange in the train, before diving behind the " Hove Herald " and the " Brighton Bugle " for the rest of the journey.

A very different bag of bails is the propagandist who stands glaring and muttering at second slip. His conversation is addressed to first slip or gully, but directed at the batsman. His observations, usually prefaced by gasps of astonishment and hisses of contempt, go something like " By gracious me, that was pretty near," or " Gaw—I thought that had taken his specs off."

An interesting variation of this propagandist type was a very keen amateur of recent years who, unlike some of his weaker brethren, never gave way to rude Anglo-Saxon words when the tide ran agin him. As his gorge rose, which it did very readily, it would pour forth words of frightening length and terms of chillingly official tone. It was said that his team could, from these symptoms, assess his blood pressure to a tee and that, when the word " transmogrification " was coupled with a threat to " report the matter to the proper authorities through the correct channels " he was about to blow his top.

But surely the most terrifying propaganda machine ever seen on the field of play must have been the brothers Grace, one at point and the other at short square leg. Woe betide the callow young batter, caught between the hammer of the spade beard and the anvil of the mutton chop whiskers.

Less venomous but more affecting than the propagandist is the Jeremiah who pauses between overs, with a shake of the head and a great rattling sigh, to say a few pale words about the sadness of it all. That he is generally to be found in the ranks of the elderly professionals is no reflection on the profession, but merely means that he has to stagger along with his burden for purely economic reasons, while the similary melancholy minded amateur has given up the struggle at an earlier date. He, poor chap, is probably crying quietly somewhere on top of the pavilion, having been eased out of the dressing room by the very captain he sought to warn of the catastrophic state of affairs about him.

Wit there has been in abundance, and I remember one sprightly exchange between two very sprightly players at Bradford many years ago. Nigel Haig took guard against George Macaulay on a wet wicket in a fourth and hopelessly lost cause. Up rushed Macaulay and out rushed Haig. The meat of the bat met the ball half volley at the end of a frenzied flailing swing. The result was quite frightening and batsman and bowler stood together in mid pitch, whence impetus had carried them, watching the spectacular flight of the ball with staring eyes. As it disappeared several streets away the striker broke the stunned silence.

"What do you know about that, George?" he asked.

Wonderment had for once quelled all indignation in that gallant man's breast.

"Ech," he replied in hushed and reverent tones, " it's a lucky thing you didn't hit it in t'middle of bat."

There is always something most admirable about the man who can jest in times of adversity and although this tale, told me by Arthur Mailey, took place on the verge of a very much wider sphere than any cricket ground, I cannot refrain from including it. You may remember that in 1921 Warwick Armstrong, having beaten England eight times in a row and fought a draw at Manchester, found himself at the Oval with another certain draw on his hands. But it was still a Test Match, and there was a good deal of criticism when he rested his regular bowlers and later took himself off to the deep field, a region for which he was conspicuously ill fitted. When a newspaper blew along and he started to read it there was real umbrage, for it was regarded as a very off-hand gesture. It must be remembered that English cricket was in a delicate state, and that no fewer than thirty English players had appeared during the Series, a point which bears on this tale.

Well, many years afterwards, when Warwick was on his death-bed, Arthur Mailey went to see him. Warwick had no illusions about his condition, but they talked of old times, and eventually Arthur said there was one thing he had always wanted to know, to which the sick man bade him ask whatever he wanted to. Arthur asked him if he remembered the newspaper incident and, being told he did, said he had always thought it a strange gesture and wondered why he had done it.

" Do you really want to know?" said Warwick.

" Yes," said Arthur. " I do."

A gleam rekindled in Warwick's eye as he tersely replied.

" I wanted to know who we were playing against."

In the ripe years of one's retirement one only learns of the wit and wisdom exchanged on the field of play second hand, but I would gather that Alec Bedser has seldom been at a loss for pleasantry or, when necessary, pungent comment. I liked the casual few words he had with Keith Miller at Sydney, following an unsuccessful appeal for lbw. " You lucky devil," he said. " That would have knocked your off stump out of the ground."

" Nonsense," replied the striker, " but it would certainly have hit the middle."

It was at Leeds against India that he had Hazare caught behind the wicket, after a fourth wicket stand of 222. It was a magnificent catch off an attempted late cut, and Godfrey Evans could not refrain from pointing out that it had been off the bottom edge. The bowler acknowledged this as a fine feat but explained in terms of some force that, on the pitch provided, it was not possible to get the ball high enough to hit the top one.

In South Africa Trevor Bailey's partners came to regard two pet phrases almost as texts for the day's struggle. One was: " Needless to say I shall be employing my usual tactics against Goddard," and the other, on the batsmen parting for their respective ends: "May good fortune attend your efforts." The last has a delightfully benedictory air, and cannot but have reassured the nervous starter.

Finally, a tribute to one of the greatest all-round cricketers and conversationalists of recent years, Brown (G.) of Hampshire and England. You may have read "Crusoe" Robertson-Glasgow's delightful account of the great man's arrival at Portsmouth, and his genial description of motor-cycling over tramlines, addressed to an astonished and fascinated spectator. Of his hearty laugh and abrupt departure, leaving the listener, who had not previously had the very great pleasure of his acquaintance, gazing after him stupefied.

I have the pleasantest memories of his striking the first ball at Lord's from very near the Tavern to very near the furthest boundary and, running five to a young but rather portly partner's three. Sometimes as they sped along abreast he would pour a stream of admonition into the young man's pink and embarrassed ear, sometimes he would dart ahead and they would meet face to face, occasionally he would fling a well turned taunt over his shoulder. No wonder the portly one left shortly afterwards.

At a Southern festival a large-footed amateur twice essayed to pick the ball up and twice kicked it before him. A great cavernous voice arose to bid him in rich Hampshire accents: "Go through on your own, Sir." And when in India the native batsmen would draw together to exchange their gentle hissing conferences they were liable to be joined by a majestic gloved figure who addressed the conference in a tongue which sounded extremely Oriental but was, I fear, intelligible to no human ear, even that of the speaker.

I would tell you more, but there are a couple of cricketers in my office and I can hardly hear myself think.

CHAPTER EIGHTEEN

The Traveller, Local

THE CRICKETER IS PERFORCE A TRAVELLER, whether it is to the neighbouring village or, rather further, to Australasia. Given good companionship, as is usually the case, the journey is a very pleasant part of the performance. For the mature it means amusement and instruction, for the young fun and bags of romance, and for the very young, perhaps best of all, extra tuck. Indeed, one of my wife's happiest memories of a very limited participation in the game of cricket is her appointment as scorer to the First XI, Royal School, Bath, who always had buns for tea.

Some school-day excursions have been less innocent. One precocious lad, later a well known county cricketer, having escaped the vigilant eye of the accompanying master, led his fellow sixteen- and seventeen-year-olds into a pub. Having satisfied the demands for lemon squash and ginger pop, he turned to the barman with a worldly air. " Mine's a large whisky," he said, "—*and make it Haig.*"

The next stage in the cricketing pilgrim's progress is university cricket, of which I have the happiest memories. On tour, however, there were few riotous occasions for competition for " Blues " was keen and the varsity match in the offing.

As fine a form of travel as I can remember was with the Middlesex team in days of yore. We had a particularly happy and entertaining company at all times, everyone a personality in his own right. There comes to mind the sayings and doings of Frank Mann, Nigel Haig, Gubby

Allen, Tom Enthoven, Walter Robins, George Newman,
Ted Carris and John Guise amidst a host of amateurs and
an equal wealth of character with pros like Joe Murrell,
Pat Hendren, Jack Hearne, Jim Smith, Jack Durston, Joe
Hulme to name a few. To this day all sorts of trivialities
bob up to keep these memories warm. As when we struck
a new, unknown and disastrous umpire, and in the home-
bound train had some harsh things to say of him. He
found a champion in the warm-hearted Patsy who cited a
number of athletic activities with which he had been connected. This kindly defence was somewhat punctured by
a good Lancastrian enquiry from Joe Hulme (one of the
victims) as to " which year did he row int' boat race?"

There is the memory, when playing against Somerset, of
Nigel Haig's return from Farmer White's poker party in
the wee small hours. In view of the Farmer's hospitality
Nigel's escort and driver, a neighbouring farmer of the
old school, had deemed it prudent to make the homeward
journey of several miles entirely in bottom gear. The
effect produced on an elderly, but invincible, little touring
car was something between the Bristolian and Mount
Vesuvius. It was here that Sam Woods sat lightly on the
ping pong table and brought the evening's play to an
abrupt and dramatic end, when it went down with a rend-
ing crash, leaving Sam impaled in several tender places by
the splinters to which it had been reduced.

The highlight of our travelling days was on August Bank
Holiday when we set course for the seaside.

In the good old days, a term that seemed particularly
appropriate to Brighton, Sussex v. Middlesex was a great
event, at least for the players. The season being well
advanced and all prospects of the championship usually
evaporated, the company drew breath for a good blow-out,
even should the expense cause the committee a good
blow up.

The amateurs stayed in a glittering hotel and we penni-
less undergraduates dined and wined amidst the rich and
affluent. There was ever incident and excitement to be

had, with the rich and affluent guests providing much of the entertainment.

Over the years comes another happy memory of the tremendously special dish which proved more of a land-mine extraordinary than a bombe surprise when the chafing dish, swollen with priceless ingredients, exploded with a bang which blew the drooling expectant fleshpots out of their chairs and the management clean out of their esteem.

There was about this time an event almost as remark-able as Sherlock Holmes's " Curious incident of the dog in the night." In this case the dog hurtled down the lift shaft from six floors up and, having crashed through the roof of the lift car at the bottom and completed three laps of the lounge undreamt of in the greyhound Derby, shot out of the door to be found next day some miles away, thoughtful but undamaged.

Annually, on the guest list was a prominent financier who obviously had had a frustrated childhood, for it was his passion to conduct the band in the grand manner. Unfortunately for him, Frank Mann considered these interludes a good opportunity to improve his own neg-lected musical education.

Taking advantage of the conductor's short sight, he would conceal himself among the instrumentalists, with the result that the maestro's finest moments were liable to be marred by the discordant blare of a trumpet, or an ill-timed thunder of drums, according to the novice's fancy of the moment.

In later years I succeeded to the captaincy and was joined by George Mann, so providing something of a link, as his father had been captain when I made my first appearance. Many of the players I first knew had by then retired, but the Middlesex family tradition continued and we travelled around most happily. In addition to George we had Bert Carris and Neil Hotchkin more or less regu-larly. Joe Murrell, so bright of eye and grand of character, was scorer and father confessor to the side and directed the education of the bridge players with a firm hand. My own travelling recreation was wrestling with crossword puzzles, and I remember once asking the company what a Rechabite might be. Joe immediately replied: "Very strict religious sect," then—darting a look at George, who is a member of the famous brewing family, "Won't touch beer." There was a pause before he peered over his cards again to sum the matter up. "Won't touch water if the pipe comes past a brewery," at which he dived into the bidding once more.

It was at Cheltenham that George unaccountably missed a number of enormously high ballooners in the deep. In the evening we went to the local Follies where dear old Davy Burnaby sang a ballad he had composed in his honour. It was entitled: "Little man you've had a missy day."

At Birmingham we lunched together with many guests at the Mayor's board where Neil Hotchkin got involved in a furious argument between two ninety-year-olds as to who had the most ancient personal connections. Curiously enough the junior, who was only ninety-three, silenced the senior by recalling that his grandfather had stood next to Sir John Moore at the battle of Corunna and felt the wind of the fatal bullet. The only other thing I recall about this match was that we departed on the third morning with the ground shrouded in fog and under about an inch of water and the secretary in a great state lest it should dry out and be fit for play. As it looked as though we should be lucky if the ground was ready for next season's match we took our departure despite his fears and protests.

But by this time the war was nearly upon us and, after a very happy first visit to Canterbury we set off on a very different sort of journey. At the end of the war I played a few matches as we struggled to get things going again but it was soon sadly apparent that my days as a playing traveller with Middlesex were over.

SCOTLAND

Cricket has taken me back to my native land quite often ; "mony a cantie day" I have had. It has occasionally struck me that people in the South have very little idea of the amount and quality of the cricket played in Scotland so perhaps I may spend a few moments on the subject.

I learnt to play cricket at Uddingston, which was then a large village some miles from Glasgow. The cricket club was a most flourishing concern, with a beautiful ground within the policies of Bothwell Castle. There was a large active membership so that it was easily possible to maintain three elevens, a junior team and a minor team. Every evening in the summer, weather permitting, there would be half a dozen nets in action and, when the weather gave but a qualified permission, there would be fielding practice.

The first eleven home matches were a considerable event. Uddingston were competitors in the Western Union, the league for major clubs in the Glasgow district, a competition which they frequently won. They were always referred to as "The Villagers" and, in days of few motor cars, and little counter attraction, a Saturday afternoon match would always draw between two and three thousand spectators. The standard of cricket was comparable to the Northern English leagues, but although the sides each had a professional they did not run to the star talent of, say, the Lancashire League. There were nonetheless some good performers and for some years Uddingston had for their pro. Irving Turner of Yorkshire, a fine player and a most popular man.

There were about a dozen clubs in the Union, which I believe is the case to-day. But The Villagers' greatest rivals in those days was Drumpellier, a club which operated some miles away at Coatbridge. Their opening batsman, C. T. Mannes, a very fine looking player, was a great scourge to rival bowlers. Despite a clubfoot he had a beautifully free style, a fine range of stroke and real power. One of my fondest of all cricket memories is going, with my father, to Hamilton Crescent in Glasgow to see Mannes go in first, with George Gunn against the Australians in 1921. They got 40 for the first wicket, quite an event against Jack Gregory. I still see that magnificent bounding run and leap, with George advancing crabwise from the opposite end, but the real high spot for me was when Gregory bowled a half volley and Mannes, then of ripe years as a batsman, thumped it straight to the screen.

Scotland's leading batsman at that time, and for many years was " Wee John " Kerr. He stood so " two-eyed " that his toes pointed past the bowler, but, predominantly a back player, he had a rock-like defence. Just after the Hamilton Crescent match he made a hundred against the Australians at Edinburgh.

Talking of Hamilton Crescent and Australians, I believe it was here that Warwick Armstrong was introduced to the Scotch whisky trade, to which he belonged for the rest of his days. At the bar he met Peter Dawson, a famous name in the trade, and in the course of conversation they got round to the question of Armstrong's impending retirement and future. Dawson suggested that he should take his Australian agency, and a very happy partnership was born. When Dawson was absorbed by the Distillers' Company, Armstrong continued as representative of James Buchanan and Company.

Four years after this meeting, Armstrong came to visit his headquarters and was roped in to play for West of Scotland against Uddingston in a Charity Cup Final. It so happened that the other opening bowler was the Rev. H. F. T. Heath, who had played for South Australia, and there were great cries of "Australia versus Uddingston." No matter, Uddingston won.

Cricket flourishes greatly round Edinburgh, but I cannot speak of it with any greater experience than one match against The Royal High School, thirty-five years ago. Wickets tend to be faster than on the humid west coast, to judge from those further to the north. I used to play a most delightful country house week's cricket with Charles Carnegie, now Southesk, around Angus. Here again the standard was high, sometimes too high for our rather gay and light-hearted approach of the visitors from the south. We played against Forfarshire when Frank Smailes was professional .and, when he went to Yorkshire, he was succeeded by Bill Andrews, who later returned to play for his native Somerset.

The Scottish Counties compete in a championship table and play is good and keen and strongly supported. On another tour I played on the North Inch at Perth, which is also a beautiful ground, by the river. It was the fastest wicket I can remember seeing in Scotland and, with the top spinner slipping through, I got four lbw's in a row, all given out by Jimmy Ferguson, an old Scottish player. The crowd gave him one or two very old-fashioned Scots words for this adherence to duty, but these he heard with manly resignation.

The team was Sir Julien Cahn's and a very good one, which was just as well for we struck some very good seam bowling from Marshall, of Notts, and Willie Anderson, Scotland's captain and a fine big, lively fast bowler. Marshall was eventually employed by A. K. Bell, also of whisky fame and a great lover of cricket, who was instrumental in engaging Wilfred Rhodes as his successor. This was in the nature of a return, for Rhodes had spent some of his early career as professional in the Border country.

Although I have taken the field in the neighbouring county of Aberdeen, for which I have a birth qualification, I have never played on the county ground. This I regret, but can boast that my father made a hundred on it the day my brother was born. However, blood is thicker than water, and just the other day I said to Peter May: " Surely I know that tie you are wearing?" to which he replied: " You should—it's Aberdeenshire." He had been presented with it on his visit last September and I recalled the colours from my father's cap.

North of Aberdeen one runs into the territory of the
Highland League, which extends from Huntly to Inverness and in which the game is most sturdily played. Ross-
shire is, so far as I know, the northernmost outpost and
numbers amongst its past players Walter Robins. Thereafter, the terrain, although the most beautiful in the world,
is hardly suitable for cricket.

The game is not only well and keenly played in Scotland but fostered and kept alive in the off-season by the
Scottish Cricket Society, a most active and energetic body.
They arrange for regular visits of famous players and
authorities to give talks and lectures, and everyone who
has had the pleasure of addressing them has been struck
by the immense knowledge and enthusiasm of the members. As I write, Denis Compton is packing his bags and
polishing up his notes in preparation for a trip to the
North.

It will be a great day when Scotland is represented in
the County Championship.

CHAPTER NINETEEN

The Traveller, Abroad

DURING THIS TIME I HAD TRAVELLED
quite extensively to and in other countries. My first major
excursion was to South Africa with the M.C.C. As I was
but eighteen, very young for my years and feckless, my
state of excitement may well be imagined as the boat train
headed for Southampton and the good ship *Kenilworth
Castle*, a fine, coal-fired, quadruple expansion, 1905
number.

We hadn't got further than the Bay when I learnt that,
whatever my shortcomings as a traveller, and they were
plenty, I had one great asset. I was a good sailor and to
this day have remained unaffected in all circumstances.
This was also to the benefit of Percy Holmes, a sailor so
fragile that a view of the sea on a movie screen was sufficient to throw his innards into a confusion. I gave him
the hyoscine pills given me by a lady doctor on my departure, and at least he was alive when we arrived at Madeira.

This was my first glimpse of a foreign country and I
have never forgotten it. In the uncanny silence of a ship
hove to after several days at sea I peered out of the port-
hole, and saw the hills behind Funchal, with the cleft
running up between them, deep green and dotted with
picturesque little houses. Though rather more thickly
populated, the scene looked to me exactly like one of the
illustrations from " The Coral Island " or " Masterman
Ready " and it remains clear in my mind's eye as I write.

This was a fitting prelude to the beauties of the Cape,
an attractive city in a lovely district. Bob Wyatt and I
stayed up all night to see the lights of Cape Town on our

arrival and I spent most of the next day falling asleep wherever I sat down. Even so I was sufficiently alert to appreciate a first view of Newlands, which I still think is the most beautiful cricket ground of all. When we arrived the glass was somewhere in the nineties and the smell of the pine trees came wafting across the shimmering field.

In a far corner was the massive figure of J. J. Kotze, at one time the fastest bowler in the world. He stood gazing lovingly at a strip of turf, an experimental grass pitch which he tended with his own hand, prodding it gently here and sprinkling a little water there. Once when he had gone to replenish his watering-can a couple of women wandered near it in their high heels, at which he came charging out of the trees, bellowing with rage and anxiety, and drove them helter skelter with menacing gestures of his can. It was difficult to say which party suffered the greatest nervous shock.

He was a great character and soon afterwards I remember a somewhat alarming drive round the mountainous coast road with him. It was alarming as there was at most points a good drop into the sea and, at all points, a long cut in one of his front tyres.

Our journey took us to all the large centres. At Johannesburg we played on the old Wanderers' ground, which looked like a vast, red, hard tennis court with a green matting wicket in the middle. This was fast and true, and provided the best game of cricket I have ever seen. It was also a good surface to field on. In later years it became a fine grass arena, after which it was acquired by South African Railways to be turned into a marshalling yard.

The only turf wicket on which we played a first class match was at Kingsmead, Durban. Even thirty years ago it was a beautiful surface and we made a lot of runs. The Test Match was, however, played on matting. As I remember it was about 107° in the shade and intensely humid but, as Durban boasts one of the finest sea fronts in the Empire, we were able to spend quite a lot of time simmering gently in the brine. The breakers come in at regular intervals in long straight lines, so that even the novice can have great fun with a surf board. The only discordant moment I can remember was when my half section, Bob Wyatt, sighted the umpire who had given him out lbw (in his opinion mistakenly) paddling peacefully in the waves. Bob decided the Indian Ocean wasn't big enough for both of them, so sat moodily on the beach.

On the homeward journey I had my entire worldly wealth, about £50, changed in golden sovereigns, which chinked delightfully in a little canvas bag. I wonder what they would be worth now. Anyway, I spent one or two of them on a green parrot at Madeira, a fine sturdy old bird, with a broken wing and a great flow of Portuguese, which we suspected was of a warm and colourful flavour. It had evidently been brought up on a farm for the rest of its repertoire was a deafening cackling, braying and crowing. Our relationship was, alas, but short, for I lived in rooms and, although my landlady didn't speak Portuguese, she was not best pleased when the farmyard burst into raucous life about five in the morning.

A second trip to South Africa followed under the captaincy of Percy Chapman in 1930-31. This time we played one Test on grass at the Cape and two on grass at Durban. The other two were on the mat at Johannesburg. Having lost the first at Jo'burg we all said: "Wait till we get them on turf." In due course we did, at Newlands, and Jack Siedle and Bruce Mitchell put up a record for the first wicket that stands to this day. The others batted pretty well too, and we were lucky to get away with a draw.

The Third Test at Durban got off to a strange start. Being one down we were on the chase, so when Percy won the toss, with a bit of wet on the pitch, he put South Africa in to bat. When we got to the middle the umpire found that the bails, designed for the smaller stumps, would not fit the larger variety. No other bails were to be found on the ground so there was nothing for it but to send someone to the nearest sports shop. All this took about twenty minutes and scarcely had we started when the rain came down again. It was irritating at the time but had little bearing on the result, which was another draw. In the evening we went to the cinema with Mr. Platt of Isipingo and three of his five lovely daughters. The youngest, Valerie, we did not meet on that occasion, she being in her cot. She is now Mrs. Denis Compton.

On this trip we got as far north as Livingstone and saw the Victoria Falls. One of the many things that cricket has brought me is a boast of having seen both the Victoria and the Niagara Falls.

It has not been my luck to see South Africa since these relatively far off days, but I have not given up hope of returning once more. Whatever its problems, of which one reads so much, it is for me a beautiful country, full of warm, hospitable people.

My cricket travels have taken me also to Ceylon, Malaya, India, Canada, America, Germany and Holland, all of which have given me good memories. These, however, I have described at length elsewhere so will not dwell on them. There also ends my journeying as a player.

To every aspiring cricketer Australia is the promised land. It used to be the batsman's paradise and as such frequently the bowler's purgatory. It has been truly said that no writer on cricket is complete in his craft until he has made a trip " down under."

It was as a writer that I made my first, but I hope not last, trip, for I never had the good fortune to go as a member of a team. In whatever capacity one goes there it is a wonderful and stimulating experience. The territory is vast, but so good are the air services, that it is possible to see a good deal of the country in the comparatively limited time at the disposal of a cricket correspondent on tour.

However, it is with the game of cricket the journalist is chiefly concerned and the beauties of nature must be a secondary, if very pleasant, feature for his observation.

The first centre we saw was Perth. It is a splendid ground with a vast playing area and a pitch, brick hard and lightning fast, in the old Australian tradition. Amidst the pleasant surroundings the only snag is a rubbish dump on one flank which, on Len Hutton's trip, produced a smoke screen of such intensity that play was stopped and the local fire chief alerted. This was somewhat unusual and generally the facilities are first class, so that, with the city rapidly expanding, Western Australia have for some time been urging their claims to a Test Match, but have not so far been successful. Those who oppose these claims do so on the grounds that the district is remote from the other large centres, and could not itself support a Test Match, in terms of gates and attendances. This objection may well disappear in the next few years, not only with the increase of Western Australia, but the acceleration of the air services to a point where Sydney to Perth will be a day trip.

When in Perth I took the field for the Governor's team. General Sir Charles Gairdner, whom I had last seen in Egypt, ran this side against schools and had until that time never lost a match. Lindsay Hassett was our star guest but, on his being out lbw in our innings, we collapsed and the Governor's proud record was shattered.

From there we journeyed to Adelaide, which is a beautiful city and boasts a ground which is never omitted in any discussion on the world's most comely cricket pitches. It again is large to English eyes, with an immense carry to the screen at either end. From certain angles it is one of the most picturesque of all grounds and awakened a fine nostalgia for me when I looked out of the stand to the distant hills, which bore a very close resemblance to those behind Inverness, as they run down to the Great Glen. There I met " Nip " Pellew, as I have described elsewhere and Jack Rymill, who made a hundred against Maurice Tate at his best.

There can be few happier or more engaging cricketers than Jack, now head of a large business organisation.

When I asked him about this feat he laughed heartily and said the one thing he could remember was returning to the dressing room very pleased with himself, and being told by Clem Hill that if he'd known just a little more about Tate he wouldn't have made ten.

Thence to Melbourne, which was another grand meeting place, where we had a reunion with the famous firm of Woodfull and Ponsford. The former introduced me to Bert Ironmonger, which was a great moment for, if I have written of him as batsman and fielder in irreverent vein, it does not mean that I have not long been a most ardent admirer. It was at Sydney, however, that I met most of the heroes of my boyhood.

There are no cricketers like the ones you saw when you were twelve years old, and the 1921 Australian was to me the greatest team of all time. Jack Ryder I had met at Perth, where he warmed my heart by remembering with obvious enjoyment the century he had made at Hamilton Crescent, Glasgow, which I had watched from various points of vantage, sometimes from between the legs of the taller spectators and sometimes from the top of the fence. Arthur Mailey was, of course, an old friend of all and had also joined us at Perth.

Warwick Armstrong, Sammy Carter, Warren Bardsley and Ted McDonald had died since those glorious days, but the survivors turned out in force to a reception for the M.C.C. on their arrival in Sydney. There was Jack Gregory, to my mind the greatest cricketer of all, with his physique, personality, thunderous action and dashing batting and slip fielding. There was Herbie Collins, Tommy Andrews, Stork Hendry and Bert Oldfield, but a notable absentee was Charlie Macartney. He is, however, still going strong.

There was also present Sydney Smith, who managed the '21 side, who made a speech. Australians are very fond of eloquence, but it was something of a surprise when above the deafening din of about two hundred fluent conversationalists the chairman, banging and bawling to make himself heard, said he was going to call on his old friend for a few words. It was obviously a lost cause from the word go but Mr. Smith battled away manfully for over thirty minutes, punctuated and supported by thumps of the gavel and despairing cries for silence. I regret to say I heard not one word of this oration, but James Swanton was luckier for he heard two. They were " Lord Hawke."

Later I had the great pleasure of dining next to Tommy Andrews, who is a great chap, and a great lover of this country. But this was characteristic of so many Australians and not least of the reasons why I am such an ardent Aussie supporter. It is a heartening and wholly delightful experience to get into an Australian taxi and hear the driver talk about " home," whether he has ever been to this country or not and whether or not he has any prospect of ever getting here. Everybody who lives in this country and loves it should know of the vast treasure house of loyalty and pride of race that exists in Australia, and everybody should do whatever lies in his power to foster it. That it is the most practical and stout-hearted loyalty does not have to be said, for it has been amply demonstrated on every possible occasion.

I thought the cricket crowds in Australia were fair and generous, though vociferous to our ideas. The Hill at Sydney seemed to me to be less partisan in outlook than one or two crowds I could name in this country. True they say some very old-fashioned things in moments of disapproval ; but these hostilities seemed to me to be equally divided between friend and foe alike. When pleased they are also uninhibited but again, from what I saw, just as demonstrative towards the successful visitor. They rose to our young batsmen, May and Cowdrey, when they made their centuries.

The next time I am in Sydney, which I hope to be this next series, I am determined to have a day on the Hill. Bill Griffith did this when he was touring there with the M.C.C. side on its way to New Zealand. He had a wonderful time. He went strictly incog. and was soon invited to join a group, whose strongest common link was a large keg of beer. The hosts did not know for some time that they were entertaining a Pommy let alone a member of the side in the middle. Every over they had a bob sweep on the number of runs scored, and Bill said that much of the barracking came from agitated speculators who feared the batsmen were going to fall short of their expectations.

Australian manners are perhaps on the whole less formal but there is a fine friendliness about the ordinary course of the day's work and play. Certain aspects of officialdom are on the other hand brusque and, to the uninitiated, overbearing. Many of us felt, after some experience, that the friendly Australian soul was allergic to a hat with a badge on it. The gateman, for instance, is not just a collector of tickets but a fearsome and baleful spider who lies in wait for the innocent little fly. If, like Denis Compton, he turns up without his " tick-ut," the spider rushes out and devours him with many terrible threats, and fearsome verbal lacerations. For if you want to travel in peace in Australia remember that to have no " tickut " is just below murder, rape and treason on the criminal code. If there happens to be an Aussie on duty when you get to the pearly gates you had better make arrangements for alternative, if less comfortable, accommodation, just in case. And don't think you will get anywhere by saying you're a pal of Don Bradman's—they've heard that one before.

I sometimes, when I had been more than usually severely ticked off for some documentary omission, asked the authorities why their officials were so fierce, at which they would laugh and say that their clients were sometimes hardly the docile, law-abiding crowds of the old country. They also said that the different sections of spectators had to be fairly definitely segregated and that, if they let spectators walk about the ground as is the custom over here, they would have little hope of getting the occupants of the free seats back to their allotted places. So, what with a sturdy and persistent pioneering spirit, anyone entrusted with the exercise of law and authority took a fairly suspicious view of all humanity. It is worth mentioning that when I sympathised with Denis over the gate-jumping incident and mentioned my own not infrequent disputes, Alec Bedser, not only a lover of Australia, but a man of great good sense, said to me in tones of some severity that, in all his days in Australia, he had never had any bother, so perhaps I exaggerate.

In any case it is a small matter compared to the hospitality shown the visitor from all other quarters. Press arrangements are on the whole first class, good, commodious press boxes and well run luncheon rooms, at the club's expense. At Perth the type of desk provided was taken as a model to be recommended to all planners in this country. It divided each writer from his neighbour by a partition similar to those in post offices for writers of telegrams. This did not prevent a fine confusion between my neighbour, Lindsay Hassett, and myself when a smart breeze sprang up to further complicate a certain lack of orderliness, so that we spent much of our first day's assignment rescuing our precious copy from each other. Next day we both turned up with a sufficient cargo of clips, pins and assorted ballast to start a stationery shop, and conducted our business like a couple of efficiency experts.

There is a tremendous amount to be said for and about Australia. As I have said, I hope to re-visit it for the next M.C.C. tour to see many old friends again and to gain many fresh impressions. My suits are all being fitted with a special fool-proof ticket pocket—just for fear any of these remarks should catch the attention of the Gate Keepers' Union.

CHAPTER TWENTY

It's an Ill Wind-up

PRACTICE AT REDTHORNE C.C. WAS OVER
for the evening and a small knot of players were discussing
their captain's new motor car. It stood behind the pavilion
shining and resplendent in the setting sun, a fitting reward
for its owner's patient years of saving and dreaming. His
companions, with the prospect of another year or two's
saving and dreaming, surveyed its glittering splendour and
enviously inquired what he thought of the new front wheel
springing layout.

Mr. Dumble, whose practical experience of motoring
was now confined to the motor mower, surveyed the
machine through the dressing-room window with his usual
Olympian serenity.

"Aye," he said at length. " Very nice, but I would sooner
have 'orse and trap meself." " Dick," said the crestfallen
owner, " you're an old stick-in-mud."

"A-ho, I've doon a bit o' motorin' in my time," said
Mr. Dumble, a reminiscent gleam coming in his eye. " In
fact, I'll tell you a story wot I hope will be a warnin' to
you.

"Woon day afore season starts," said Mr. Dumble, "I
were taking dog for walk when round t'corner cooms chap
int great coat and goggles. Wot with gauntlets on his
'ands and his cap on back to froont he looks a proper sight
and dog starts to go mad.

" ' Dick,' says chap, ' for goodness sake keep that dampt
mongrel o' yours under control—you'd think 'ed never
seen a 'uman being afore.'

" And he takes off his goggles and it's Mr. Borrington
wot were our skipper.

" 'Well,' I says, 'To tell the truth I was a bit nervous meself, wot with reading this new-fangled chap named Wells. Wots t'game?'

" 'Coom with me,' says skipper. 'I'll show you summat very special.'

" So we walks round corner to a chap named Knockins who keeps garage nearby and skipper fishes int pocket and starts to unlock big red door. He throws it open with a great flourish and theers biggest motor you ever saw.

" 'Well, Dick,' he says. 'Wot do you think o' that?'

" I'm dumbfounded, but dog 'as no doubt about 'is feelings. He gives woon piercing yelp and disappears out of yard with 'is tail between 'is legs.

" 'That's a very timid beast o' yours,' says skipper, very impatient. 'You can't be feeding it right.'

But I'm not sure meself that dog isn't wise. Motor's got two big brass lamps in froont and a great horn made to look like a serpent that coils over mudguard. It's at least eight feet 'igh and ont radiator theers very fancy German name, like Poffle-Flugwagen.

" 'Isn't she a beauty, Dick?' says skipper. 'Look at t'lines of 'er—dormant, irresistible power. She might be a live thing,' he says. 'A panther ready to spring.'

" 'How did you coom by this?' I says, tryin' to 'umour 'im.

" 'Well, as a matter of fact,' he says, 'I won 'er int raffle.'

" 'Int raffle?' I says.

" 'Aye,' he says, 'You remember a chap named Troutley wot played a few times for Bailshire? He had 'er last. But of course you can't have a magnificent machine like this for long without attracting soom attention—especially from police. So every time he takes her out theers soom trouble, and it gets so expensive that he decides, very relooctant, to get rid of 'er. We're staying into same party last week so he sells me a ticket for raffle and three days ago, after Bailton Races, we drew it and I woon. It were a wunnerful bit o' luck.'

" Well, I can see she's a bit old and been treated pretty rough and I think theers maybe been a few other expenses apart from police.

" ' How much were tickets?' I says.

" ' Five pounds a time,' he says. ' Given away you might say.'

" It seems to me if this chap Troutley has sold half a dozen tickets he's doon pretty well, but I says nowt cos skipper's fallen into kind of a trance.

" ' It'll be wunnerful this season,' he says. ' You can see us skimming swift and silent through the summer coontryside on our way to knock t'blocks off Bailshire. No waiting for trains or cabs, just a quick turn of t'starting handle and magic carpet's ready to waft us coomfortable and effortless to ends of t'earth.'

" He gives handle a twirl and theers a tremendous bang as she backfires and chooks 'im int pile o' empty petrol tins.

" Well, skipper goes crazy about motor which is known int side as ' Stonewall Bannerman ' cos it's a long time between roons. By a merciful providence it doesn't go well enough to take side anywheer for first few matches, but week afore Bailshire match skipper coomes to me in a great state of excitement.

" ' Dick,' he says. ' She's going like a bird o' paradise wot with this new carburettor, poetry o' motion you might say. We can get five int back and two int front. It's only thirty-five miles to Bailton so if we start at 9 o'clock int morning we'll be in nice time for start at 'alf past eleven. It's all arranged and we'll meet at my place. It's reet bad luck ont other four who'll have to take bags ont train but we can't get everyone in.'

" He's that keen that I haven't the 'eart to tell him how cheerful t'other four will be about their bad luck and, as nobody likes to offend 'im we all turn oop ont morning.

" Theers Captain Picklethwaite-Spelby, Bert Trimble, Bill Shackle and a coople of others, along o' skipper and meself and when we've had a mug o' ale for t'road we go out to get int motor.

" ' Would you like to sit in froont with me, Algy?' says skipper to Captain Picklethwaite-Spelby.

" ' No thanks,' says Captain. 'As you can't roon cricket side without Dick at your elbow we'd be happier if you had him theer when you're rooning motor.'

"And skipper says wot would he know about rooning anything, him being a simple soldier, so everyone's in good spirits and we climbs oop. Captain Spelby blows a tally-ho ont coaching horn he's brought along, and off we goes.

" Motor roombles along very nice for about ten miles till we get to a village ont borders of Loamshire and skipper's just saying how he's going to enter her for trials when season's doon when theers a nasty spitting, hissing noise and she stops dead. Skipper gets down and opens bonnet and peers in. In a coople of minutes half village is breathing ont back of 'is neck peering in too but nobody seems to know what's 'appened. Presently someone says:

" ' Send for t'blacksmith. He knows all about motors.'

" So blacksmith cooms and peers in at ingine and asks a lot of very 'igh sounding questions.

" ' Aye,' he says, nodding his 'ead very wise. 'As I feared it's yon new-fangled carburettor you've got on 'er. You'll have to push her along to my shop and I'll have it off and adjoost it.'

" So we all gives a shoove and blacksmith starts to work.

" ' How long will it take you?' says skipper.

" ' Maybe an hour, maybe more,' says blacksmith.

" ' Oh dear,' says skipper, ' That's very awkward. Is theer a telephone handy?'

" ' Theers one int big house what belongs to Mr. Sopson,' says smith. ' He'll let you use it.'

" ' I know Mr. Sopson,' says skipper. ' His son had a few games with second XI. We'll go right oop.'

" Mr. Sopson's theer with his wife and daughter and they make us very welcome and skipper explains wots happened.

" 'We'll be very late I'm afeared,' he says, ' but I'll speak to old Macsnayle, their captain, and maybe he'll be reasonable and delay start.'

" When Mr. Macsnayle 'ears wots happened he says it's reet bad luck.

" 'Do you think you could delay start for about an hour?' says skipper.

" ' No,' says old Macsnayle. ' We can't do that.'

" ' Well,' says skipper, stroogling with his feelings, ' We've got four players theer. Could you let us have a few substitutes till we coom?'

" ' No,' says Mr. Macsnayle. ' We couldn't do that. It would be making a farce of things.'

" Skipper gets proper steamed oop at that and calls 'im a ruddy old twister and a good many other things too, but Macsnayle won't budge.

" 'You know rules,' he says. ' If your side's not here at appointed time we shall claim match. We'll warn people of this unfortunate possibility. When you turn oop we might consider playing you a friendly match so as not to disappoint you. Goodbye just now.'

" We're in a reet tangle and no one knows what to do next till Miss Sopson speaks oop.

" ' We can't be doon by that nasty old Macsnayle,' she says. ' I've got an idea.'

" Everyone smiles a bit wry at this, and she says:

" ' My brother Oswald is on tour just now with Loam-shire Lumps,' she says, ' and at moment they're staying at Grand Hotel, Bailton. They're playing Bailshire Bum-kins this afternoon. I'll phone Oswald and tell him to take six of his best players with him and go to County Ground. With your four at least you will get a side out field and then anything might happen, it might rain. Anyway, they're not too bad and at worst we'll go down with flying colours.'

" After soom discussion we all agree that it's not a bad idea and a lot better than being blackmailed out of t'match. So Miss Sopson gets on telephone and talks to 'er brother.

" ' Oswald,' she says, ' Your county needs you. T'honour of Loamshire is entirely in your hands.'

"And she explains situation and her brother says they'll do their darndest and after that dirty trick their strength will be redoubled. Then skipper gets ont phone and gives him a lot of instroocions about delaying toss as long as possible and says if they have to play we'll play for his team int afternoon.

" When we've said our goodbyes and got back to smithy it's 'alf past ten and still twenty-eight miles to go but car's ready so we've still a chance.

" ' She'll be all right now,' says smith. ' Everything's doon and I've loosened your brakes, wot were a bit tight.'

" We go thoondering along at a tremendous speed but when it cooms to half-past eleven we're just ont outskirts of Bailton.

" You mind when you coom over last hill, theers Bailton down below with cricket ground facing you right at bottom of road, which is very steep though straight enough. Well, we shoot over crest like rocket, but way down int distance we can see that game's started to time.

" ' Too late,' says skipper. ' He's doon us, blast 'im. We needn't hurry any more.'

" He tries to slow motor down but nothing 'appens and we go faster than ever.

" ' Great Heavens!' cried skipper. ' What on earth has that village idiot doon? Brakes are busted!'

" He heaves and strains ont levers but motor keeps gathering speed and at last in desperation he says:

" ' I'll try and change 'er down—it's our last hope.'

" When theers been a terrible grinding noise I can see that he's lost all control and theers nowt but hold on and pray. Skipper tootles ont horn and I waves me red handkerchief and chaps behind are hollerin' and shouting, and all time motor is thoondering along like fire ingin. Aboove t'din I can 'ear Captain Picklethwaite-Spelby's great military voice booming out.

" 'Steady theer everyone," he shouts. 'Keep calm. Remember Waterloo,' he says. 'No faint 'earts at Balaclava.'

" Then he sticks troompet out of t'window and starts sounding t'alarm at top of 'is loongs. I think meself he might as well try Last Post, cos it's certain we can't make corner at bottom of t'hill and we're headin' straight for main gates of ground. But policeman ont gate must be old soldier cos at sound of troompet he sees us coomin' and acts very rapid. He throws gates wide open and rooshes inside, clearing folk out of t'road. Next moment we're through main gate like cannon ball going that fast that everything's blurred. Theers a fearsome crack as we go through screen like clown through paper hoop and we're out ont field with players rooning for dear life.

" 'We're all right now,' shouts skipper. 'We can go round boundary for t'rest of day if need be.'

" But guy rope from screen has got tangled round back axle and suddenly wheel locks and we do a great slithering skid and coom to rest right int middle of t'wicket.

" Rest of us are shook very bad, but Captain Spelby blows a last 'tally-'o' ont troompet and steps out cool as you like.

" 'Morning all,' he says. 'Oompire, middle and leg if you please.'

" But Mr. Macsnayle is in no mood for jokes. As soon as he's recoovered sufficient he cooms rooning at skipper demented.

" 'You dampt scoundrel,' he says, shakin' his fist at 'im. 'You've doon this a purpose.'

" And he carries on like he's going to have t'apoplexy till Captain Spelby says if he's impugning t'honour of Loamshire he'd best be ready to give immediate satisfaction. Groundsman's wringing his 'ands and crying like child and policeman's taking noomber of t'car. In midst of hub-bub I see Mr. Oswald Sopson so I draws 'im aside and has a word in his ear. So he waits until they've cooled Mr. Macsnayle down till he's in no more than a state of oongovernable passion and he steps oop to 'im very official.

"'I'm very sorry, Macsnayle,' he says. 'But you know rules. Pitch has been tampered with so I'm afraid we shall have to abandon match.'

"At that Mr. Macsnayle starts off agin, but Bailshire secretary steps in.

"'Gentlemen,' he says. 'Let us retire to the privacy of committee room and discuss matter calmly.'

"Well, president of club, t'Earl of Bailshire, is a reet good sport and when he's heard story he laffs very 'earty and says the great matter is that no one has been hurt. When all's said and doon by half-past twelve we've re-started match with our full side and everyone's quite happy—or anyway 'most everyone.

"Int evening we stand Loamshire Lumps the finest dinner 'otel can provide and when port 'as gone round a few times skipper says a few words o' thanks for their help.

"'I'm very pleased to say,' he says, just afore he sits down, 'that I am in a position to do you all a turn in exchange. For the nominal charge of 10/- each,' he says, drawing boondle from his pocket, 'I am prepared to give each of you a ticket in a raffle. The first prize,' he says, 'is a most magnificent, valuable and historic motor car.'"

CHAPTER TWENTY-ONE

Attire and Insignia

"I HAVE VERY SELDOM MET WITH A CRICK-
eter of eminence who did not . . . impress upon his tailor
the momentous importance of comfortably fitting clothes."
So wrote Dr. Grace in the Badminton Book of Cricket,
published in 1888. By that date cricket attire, and cricket
gear in general, had progressed through various stages and
differed only in detail from that worn at present.

A painting in the possession of the M.C.C. of a match
played about 1740 shows the players in what looks to be
a very sensible and comfortable rig. They wear loose
shirts, knee breeches, and what looks like a jockey cap.
But it seems that certain details of this dress were hardly
suitable for the purpose as one reads of John Wells tearing
off a finger-nail on his buckled shoe, in making a spectacular catch.

A picture of the England Eleven almost exactly 100
years later shows a uniformity of white flannel, but a division of policy in means of suspension. While Alfred Mynn
sports a leather belt round his manly middle, Fuller Pilch
and several others rely on wide cloth braces. All wear
collars and either bow ties or cravat, but there is a great
diversity of headgear. Messrs. Mynn and Pilch wear a
form of truncated topper, light coloured in the case of the
former, but funereal black for the latter. There are a
number of full scale toppers, but Clarke and Felix sport
cloth caps with ample peaks and loose crowns. Boots are
uniformly black leather.

The Cricket Match, painted by W. J. Bowen about five
years later, shows two of the players wearing white bowlers,

surely not a very becoming fashion, and seemingly the last innovation before the cricket cap became universal. Amongst the early caps the pill box was popular in some circles and was worn by A. G. Steel and the Hon. Alfred Lyttelton amongst others in the eighties. It must have been more ornamental than useful in sunny weather and was, presumably, exchanged for a sun hat when the wearer wanted to shade his eyes.

Perhaps the last occasion when the pill box was worn in public was on the third day of a Middlesex and Warwickshire match which had petered out to a certain draw. In the dressing room at Lord's there was a collection of ancient caps and, to brighten an otherwise dull day, the Middlesex amateurs took the field in them, headed by Nigel Haig in what must have been the most venerable specimen of the collection. It was not a very popular jest in certain quarters.

Boots to match this early type of cap were usually white, but bound with brown or black leather in the " co-respondent " style. Shirts varied between the stiff boiled front and fairly modern flannel. Collars and ties still persisted and must have been pretty trying when the score and the thermometer rose to abnormal heights. Males seem to have been much more fussy about exposing their necks than females, and some never wholly surrendered to the open-necked shirt. I seem to remember that Wilfred Rhodes, to the end of his career, wore his shirt buttoned or studded right up.

Even more conservative was Lord Harris who used to bat in the nets arrayed in boiled shirt. His nephew, the aforesaid Nigel Haig, used to describe a frightening scene when two highly nervous young lads were called upon to bowl at him. One, blind with panic and, mistaking a request for guard for the old-fashioned stance, let fly before his lordship was ready, and landed a full toss smack on his front stud. Had he been an embryonic Bradman the lad's career and nervous stability could not have survived this unintended blasphemy.

By the nineties the cricket uniform seems to have reached its determined form and, as I have said, a group of the Gentlemen of 1898 differs only in detail from that of 1958. Trousers were rather narrower in the leg. Sashes were worn round the waist and caps were tighter on the skull and smaller in the peak. The polo-necked sweater was in vogue and a very sensible garment it was for the bowler. It has since been revived for everyday use and might well reappear on the cricket field, for it supplies warmth just where it is most needed, in the neck and shoulders. Boots were now invariably white buckskin, but generally heavier than the county cricketer of today would care to carry on his feet. Here let me say that, from hard personal experience, nothing is a greater handicap to the young bowler or fielder than heavy feet. I was advised to have thick soles and several pairs of socks when young and suffered greatly until George Geary, in South Africa, lent me a pair of his very lightly made boots. If I were starting again I would certainly experiment with shoes, which I believe would not only make for better movement, but would be much less tiring.

Caps and blazers in various club colours go back to the seventies but the practice, now common to every county, of wearing the club's insignia on the sweater is comparatively recent. It originated in 1920 when Oxford University had the crowns emblazoned in dark blue on their chests in addition to the trimming round the neck. Middlesex followed this practice in 1929, if I remember rightly, with their three scimitars, and must have been about the first county to be so adorned.

The cricket tie is almost as important an item in the sartorial scale as the sacred old school tie, and also dates back quite a long way. Mr. J. G. Osborn of the old Oxford firm of Castell, a great authority on such matters, believes that all club ties originated in the eighties when a college crew, in the elation of victory, took the coloured hat bands off their boaters and tied them round their necks. In an old ledger in his possession there is an entry, dated June

25, 1880, which reads "Ribbon to straw hat 2/6" and "Ribbon Tie 1/6," supplied to a member of Exeter College.

Most of the original cricket ties are striped, I.Z., M.C.C., Foresters, Harlequins, Quidnuncs and a host of others. The number of colour combinations, or at least presentable combinations, is not unlimited, so in modern times there has been a great swing to the patterned tie with the device displayed on a more or less plain background. This is known professionally as the jaquard tie, and gives great scope for ingenuity. One of the better designs in my possession is the Wine Trade cricket tie. Originally it was a dark blue tie with small bunches of red grapes and tiny yellow wickets. Recently, the club has widened its activities and it has been necessary to add other implements which, to my mind, rather spoil the original pattern.

The England tie, for players who have played in a Test Match at home, is a particularly nice looking one with the three lions surmounted by the crown on a dark blue background. Owing to the restrictions on the use of the royal insignia for sporting purposes, however, it must only be worn on important cricket occasions, and although quite suitable for wear in the city, cannot be used to impress the clients or customers. I bought one the other day and not only had to establish my identity but had to sign a book as though dabbling in deadly poison.

I once said to Lindsay Hassett, a sports outfitter by trade, that an Australian tie on the same lines, with their crest on the green background, would make a much more attractive effect than the present green with the yellow stripe. Whether my suggestion was in any way responsible for his enterprise or not I do not know, but at a later date he had a large consignment made to this design. The result was first class, but the Australian authorities had other ideas and it was not accepted as the official tie. Lindsay very kindly sent me one, which I greatly treasure and, indeed, wear locally, if with a rather guilty air as I am not entitled to it, and sometimes wonder if the gift was not in the nature of a reminder and reproach for sticking my neck out in the first place.

The M.C.C. touring tie is a somewhat startling affair, being red, yellow and blue in narrow stripes. It would be much improved if the stripes were widened but this is presumably impossible as it would then be almost indistinguishable from the red, yellow and black of the I Zingari. This not very attractive tie is in strong contrast to the accompanying M.C.C. touring blazer which, in plain blue with red and gold piping and St. George in white on the pocket, is the best cricket blazer I know.

It is curious that at one time there was a convention which forbade the wearing of the M.C.C. tie. The reason for this ban is obscure for, although the colours are on the bright side, they are no more garish than many others. It seems that this prejudice has now largely disappeared and the tie is sported by many members, as well it might be in view of its most honourable associations. Despite W.G.'s example the cap is very rare indeed.

When considering the subject of this chapter I took a look through the remains of my cricketing wardrobe. There was an England cap which had obviously been, for some years, a welfare state for moths. There was enough of it left, however, to remind me that, in its hey-day, it was a much more resplendent affair than the modern utility model, for the insignia was worked in gold and silver thread, and the crown properly embossed. The blazer was in slightly better shape, but its dimensions had lagged behind those of its owner. There was an Oxford blazer which had seen a second lease of life for, in immediate post-war years, when no coupons were available for such frivolities, it reappeared in the 'Varsity match on the person of Ron Maudsley. There were many and assorted ties but, to the Aberdonian eye, perhaps the pick of the bunch was the plain Oxford dark blue.

It is not only a sporting tie, but eminently suitable for wear on all business and social occasions—from board meetings to funerals.

CHAPTER TWENTY-TWO

Benefits

IN 1920 JAMES SEYMOUR OF KENT WAS
given a benefit as a reward for his good services to his
county over many years. The amount involved was a sum
of about £1,000, not a vast amount to modern eyes, but
enough to attract the attention of a local Income Tax
Inspector. This conscientious official, drawing a bow at
a venture, if one may apply the phrase to one so methodi-
cal, ordained that these takings were taxable and demanded his share forthwith. Seymour very naturally
resisted this claim, and battle was joined on a principle
of great importance to every professional cricketer. The
day was eventually won by the logic and eloquence of
Lord, then Sir John, Simon, who clearly demonstrated that
a cricketer's benefit was a free gift from his employers and
admirers, and therefore beyond the grasp of the tax
collector.

The main question has not been disputed since that
time, but an interesting case arose when Bruce Dooland
left the Lancashire League, in which it is customary to put
the hat round for the professional when he has done a good
job. In Dooland's case he was entitled under his contract
to take a collection if he made 50 or took a given number
of wickets. The tax authorities deemed the money from
such collections was liable to tax, and Dooland resisted,
winning his case before Mr. Justice Harbinson. The Com-
missioners appealed and the case was then heard before
the Master of the Rolls, Lord Evershed, with Lord Justices
Birkett and Jenkins. The first two, both being very keen
cricketers, heard the case with much sympathy but, ironic-

ally enough, found it necessary to upset the previous verdict. The decision was, I believe, based on the fact that the right to take a collection was mentioned in the contract, and was therefore part of his emoluments as opposed to a free gift. The proceedings were much enlivened by Lord Birkett's comments, and he must have found this one of his more painful decisions.

But despite freedom from taxation a cricket benefit is a pretty hazardous undertaking. Nowadays there is much organisation of social functions, Sunday matches and such like to augment the general fund, but the beneficiary is still mostly dependent on the gate of the match allotted to him. In this most counties meet the desires of the player concerned in his choice of match. Not all players are as lucky as Cyril Washbrook, who was given the Australian match at Old Trafford in 1948. The result in his case was an all-time record of £14,000. Alec Bedser and Denis Compton ran this close, both having collected over £12,000. I remember running into Alec in his benefit year, after he had bowled the Australians out twice at Trent Bridge and surpassed Syd Barnes' haul of 189 wickets for England. I asked him which of the few unbroken records he was now after, at which his eye twinkled and he said: " Cyril Washbrook's would come in very handy." Well, he didn't do so badly.

At the other end of the scale there are many tales of woe. Perhaps the most heroically borne was the lot of poor old Dick Burrows who bowled so manfully over the years for Worcester. The Clerk of Weather's reward for this faithful service was three days' rain and, when the balance of takings and expenses were totted up, the " beneficiary " was only 13/4d. out of pocket. When a distressed Committee asked him if he would like another benefit Dick replied, without trace of rancour, " No thanks—I can't afford it." I knew him well in later life, which was in no way eased for him by this disaster. He never complained but dismissed all adversity with a jest and, in short, like so many of his age and type, was the salt of the earth. The greatest "benefit" bestowed upon him was a great heart and a vast sense of humour.

Alec Skelding, a similar character with an almost parallel career for Leicester, met with but meagre material reward in his benefit match. Describing this somewhat ill-starred fixture, Alec, a man with a turn of phrase, said: " Play commenced before a keen wind." George Geary, a great bowler for England and Leicester, was also unlucky.

Middlesex have always been rather favourites amongst the beneficiaries and have figured in several of the major successes, notably that of Roy Kilner who held the record until the second war. He received upwards of £4,000 from the Yorks v. Middlesex match at Leeds in 1925. Before that the greatest sum, just under £4,000, had gone to his fellow-Yorkshireman, George Hirst, who chose the Lancashire match of 1904.

The first benefit match I played in was Ted McDonald's at Old Trafford in 1929. The chief incident which sticks in my mind was the arrival of the beneficiary at the wicket and my unsuccessful efforts to "get him off the mark." A series of full tosses to leg he missed by a good margin, and a half stifled appeal for a certain lbw was answered by Nigel Haig from mid-off who said "Not out, you bloody fool" in stentorian tones. When Ted eventually got a touch and a single all he said was " Thanks—I don't want any help," which was a trifle churlish, considering what iron in my soul it was, at twenty years old, to refrain from knocking his castle over out of hand.

Next year we had Maurice Tate's benefit at Hove, and I have described elsewhere how this came to an end in two days, when one cover leaked and one did not. The resulting two-faced pitch was a problem the batsmen never looked like solving.

The last benefit match in which I took part was played against Sussex for my old friend and colleague Jim Sims. It has a rather sad memory for me. Jim presented us all with a most efficient and elegant lighter, complete with initials, to mark the occasion, and, being very prone to lose personal belongings, I took enormous care of this much treasured memento. Some years afterwards I played in a charity match and, on returning to the dressing room, found a thief had made a clean sweep of all our movables. Everyone loathes a thief at all times, but when it comes to filching objects which are patently of much sentimental value it is bumping along the bottom of all decency. If this should catch the eye of the gentleman who removed our belongings, which is unlikely, may I express the hope that things have gone very badly for him ever since, and that any function arranged for his benefit will turn out to be a major flop.

On the other hand, to all cricketers with benefit matches before them, I wish unprecedented prosperity.

CHAPTER TWENTY-THREE

Yorks and Surrey

IN THE FOREGOING CHAPTERS I HAVE OCCA-
sionally drawn comparisons between the time in which I
played and the present, in which I watch. These comparisons have been largely between differences in international cricket, as it seems Test Matches now occupy such
an enormous part of the cricket scene. The other day a
very interesting discussion arose which provided a splendid
and more particular yardstick of the pre- and post-war eras.
Someone started to speculate on the relative merits of pre-
war Yorkshire and post-war Surrey, taking both teams at
fullest strength, the Yorkshiremen to be selected from the
days of the earlier thirties when Verity and Bowes were
established and Sutcliffe still opened for England.

The first point to strike the student is the number of
similarities between the two sides. Both are supreme
amongst county sides, well and energetically led and extremely good in the field. In attack the new ball is equally
well used by Bowes and Macaulay of old and Bedser and
Loader to-day. Spin is divided between off-breakers and
left-handers in both cases and no leg-break bowler is seen
in either era. Tactics are very much alike but these may
be discussed with the other features of the out-cricket in
greater detail a little later on.

In batting, despite the presence of May, Yorkshire have
a very apparent advantage. In the thirties a Yorkshire batting order was a tough proposition, very high class for
half the way and very stubborn lower down. Holmes, Sutcliffe, Mitchell, Barber, Leyland had all played for England as batsmen in a period of fair abundance. Arthur
Wood was an appalling thorn in the flesh of many hitherto

triumphant bowlers, throwing into the battle a workman-like technique, a fine measure of guts and nous, and a slice of good luck which Jim Sims, in a moment of great heat, described as "remarkable." Brian Sellers was a most dangerous late-middle batsman who could drive home an early advantage or, when his side was in difficulties, could stage a very judicious counter-attack. The batsmen all knew their business and were able players of the turning ball, with the possible exception of the leg-break on quicker wickets. This form of bowling they distrusted as being uncertain and uneconomical (very rightly on the slow wickets of their native county) but it did mean that some of their members were unfamiliar with it when called upon to face it.

Surrey can hardly match the first half of the order and have no advantage in the later stages. In the matter of batting the advantage must clearly be with Yorkshire of the thirties.

The bowling makes a most fascinating study when looked at in greater detail. Both sides are led by champions. During the period with which we are concerned, Bowes was the best seamer in England, day in and day out. His immense height gave him a steep awkward flight, with corresponding rise from the pitch, while giving a certain disguise to his pace. He made the ball move a shade either way, keeping length and direction very tight at all times. True, he did not exploit the turning pitch as Alec Bedser can with his cut from the leg, but this was not expected of him at any time. Bedser's merits are fresh in everybody's mind so they do not call for any comment ; but it is fair to say that the sides were equally served by their opening bowler.

The opposite numbers would probably be Macaulay and Loader, a not dissimilar pair with a yard or so's pace in the latter's favour. Should the balance lie slightly in favour of the South the factor of damaged wickets this time is wholly to Yorkshire's advantage. Macaulay was a devastating off-spinner when the ball bit, and although of vastly different type, comes into comparison with Laker in this sphere. This comparison must be confined to their effectiveness in various conditions, in view of their different methods, Laker being barely medium-pace with some flight and an abundance of spin as against the Yorkshire man's fast-medium level trajectory, with an adequate amount of spin. Given helpful conditions, Laker can well claim to be one of the finest off-spinners of all time, but I doubt if George Macaulay would have been much less effective on the loose-topped wickets of recent years. On plumb wickets the off-spinner is largely at a discount, but Macaulay could then revert to a very lively fast-medium stock bowler.

The last department in the regular attacks lies between the left-handers, Verity and Lock. On turning wickets there is little to choose, as Lock's greater life and venom may offset Verity's mathematical accuracy, but, because of his command, Verity was a remarkably useful bowler on hard wickets, and able to maintain an end for long periods. Lock has not so far proved himself as a hard wicket bowler, but may soon have the opportunity to do so.

Both sides gave their bowlers the maximum support in the field, and here the scales are level.

Sellers and Surridge are curiously alike in the thrusting, determined way they lead. I don't see either side going down for lack of morale, nor do I see one gaining any tactical advantage, apart from toss or weather.

If I were a gambling man my money would be on Yorkshire, because of their advantage as a batting side, and possibly a greater versatility of attack. A very shrewd friend says he would back Yorkshire under the old lbw law and Surrey under the new, chiefly on account of Jim Laker. Perhaps in a Utopian Batter's Castle we shall be able to test out our opinions. Meantime, as so many enthralling cricket discussions, this one must remain in the realm of speculation, however firm opinions may be at Bramall Lane or the Oval. The likeliest reward for the outside speculator is a black look from both quarters.

CHAPTER TWENTY-FOUR

Around the Grounds

EARLY IN THIS BOOK I SAID THAT CRICKET
had been particularly kind to me. Having ranged through
those many topics and memories I am ready to repeat this
statement, and once again to say my very heartfelt thanks.
For one of the many boons the game has given me I am,
and should be, specially grateful ; I played for Middlesex whose home ground is Lord's. True, Middlesex are
not the owners, being tenants of M.C.C., but they are the
most frequent users, and Lord's without Middlesex is an
impossible thought.

Every boy who plays cricket in any part of the world
wants to play at Lord's. It is called " The Mecca of
cricket," a title originally bestowed in solemn idolatry, but
now used more flippantly. It is, in fact, not an inapprop-
riate one for it is the most famous cricket ground in the
world, and the M.C.C. occupies a unique position amongst
cricket clubs, and indeed amongst sporting bodies. The
Club's powers are certainly very much less than is generally supposed ; but its influence is immense.

The history of the ground is well documented, but not
everyone knows that it owes its existence indirectly to
" Bonnie Prince Charlie " and the '45. Lord's father was
a Yorkshire Jacobite, and it was in consequence of the
losses to his fortune during the uprising that his son came
to London to seek his. His original site is now Dorset
Square, and his second the railway sidings outside Maryle-
bone Station. His present one dates from 1814 ; the turf
had accompanied him, rolled up like a carpet, from his
first ground, thus the grass of Lord's was that of Dorset

Square, until the " leather-jacket " disaster and the extensive re-seeding in 1934. This may have been a blessing in disguise, for the turf is now better than I have ever seen it before. In the late twenties and early thirties the playing area could be very rough in dry weather, later on in the season. In the last century it had a name for being a pretty fiery wicket.

The slope from the north side to the south is very considerable, and the drop naturally varies with the points of measurement. So far as the playing area is concerned, the most picturesque measurement is quoted by Sir Pelham Warner, who says it is equal to a tall man wearing a top hat, about 6 feet 6 inches. The slope has, in my experience, quite an influence on the behaviour of the ball, and it is easier to turn it down the slope than against ; which is surprising in view of the very slight inclination, as seen in the middle. Like all grounds largely surrounded by stands it is not always easy for the out-fielder to see the ball immediately off the bat and, in doubtful light, the absence of a screen at the pavilion end is some handicap to the batsman, though not really a serious one.

First reactions to Lord's are not unexpectedly varied. The late Alan Fairfax once told me that when he played his first match for the Australians against M.C.C. in 1930, his first impression was that the ground was empty, so silent was the crowd. As there were nigh 30,000 of them it was a tribute to their good behaviour. Walter Brearley, a great Lancastrian and latterly a great upholder of Lord's, is said, when young and but slightly acquainted, to have enquired of an august secretary whether he was " manager of this 'ere blooming 'ippodrome." An American visitor wanted to know why M.C.C. flew the red and gold flag of Spain.

The membership is enormously varied. Again it is much more democratic than many people think. The numbers are now over 8,000, including associate members, and comprise all manner of people from the great and grand to ordinary folk, all bound together by a common love.

The pavilion and the museum are a great treasure-house of cricket relics, paintings and historical pieces. All these are in the most competent charge of the Curator, Miss Diana Rait-Kerr, daughter of Col. R. S. Rait-Kerr, an ex-secretary of M.C.C., and contribute much to the atmosphere of Lord's, unique amongst cricket grounds of the world. But it is, of course, the people concerned who make the success or otherwise of any institution. Lord's, as the home of the M.C.C., has been well served by generations of men of character and integrity, who have given time and much hard work to the affairs of the Club, without thought of personal gain. They may be cautious and, being human, occasionally ultra-reserved or even misguided, but the charges of being stuffy and snobbish which arise from the jaundiced and envious, can be forgotten. Amongst the members and officials and players there has always been a fine rich vein of character, even eccentricity. Just the other day I complained to a friend that there seemed to be less room for individuality and eccentricity in these harsh, real times, to which he rather rudely warned me to be careful, saying that quite likely, with the march of time, I had assumed the role at which I used to laugh. Although I could hardly accept this sally as being in any way possible, I couldn't but reflect that, if in years to come, I contributed something to the general fund of amusement I ought not to grudge it.

Still, I would rather not be quite so spectacular as the gentleman who, in protest at the formal dress at the Eton and Harrow match, went into the professionals' room and divested himself of everything bar his boots and grey topper. Fortunately or unfortunately, according to one's outlook, he was intercepted on the threshold of the door and his dramatic public appearance.

There was a venerable member who, on frequent visits from his native Ireland, wore the ground staff out by his prolonged practice, morning and afternoon. The bowlers, grown stale and weary in his service, hatched a plot to disable him, and so gain a little respite. An inswinger of smartish pace was selected to bowl to him on his next morning appearance, and was successful in scoring eighteen direct hits on his left boot. There was great jubilation when word went round in the afternoon that the owner was now unable to get it on to his much expanded foot. But they had underestimated their man. For his prolonged afternoon knock he merely added an extra sock to compensate for the absent boot.

A great figure at the nets in the old days was Walter Brearley who, as I have said, strictly belongs to Old Trafford, but in later years became "naturalised" to Lord's. He was said to be able to leap over a billiards table from a standing start. No one would have been unduly astonished had he leapt clean over the pavilion. He was a great bowler, but could not have been as fast as his own estimation, for to be so must inevitably have led to police intervention. Nonetheless, in after years when he had transferred his headquarters to Lord's he could still achieve a very smart pace, and was still a most awkward proposition off the 21-yard mark—a concession he accorded himself to compensate for advancing years. When the practice wickets were bone hard and rather worn he was not exactly popular, and had one particular victim. This man, who had always had a morbid aversion to anything quicker than medium pace, had for some reason attracted the full blast of Walter's generous affections and, as a result, his services as a practice bowler. The wretched man, having tried every avenue of escape, eventually made the furtive journey to the nursery via the Tavern instead of the normal grandstand route. To no avail—he arrived to find a beaming Walter pulling off his sweater and all set to "chook 'im oop a coople." Thereafter the batsman relied solely on match practice.

There was a day when "Pete" Perrin sat on the long room table with Ronnie Aird. A majestic president swept by with a patrician "Good morning, Perrin," to which Pete returned a sprightly "Morning, me Lord." Then, turning to Ronnie with an air of great satisfaction, "There y'are," he said, "nice 'owd'ya'do—and soup for the kids."

For years at the pavilion door stood a venerable scholar, whose avidity for study had just slightly disturbed his equilibrium. It was his self-appointed duty to console the unsuccessful batsman with a penny bar of chocolate, not always, I fear, a very apt or much appreciated form of compensation. Another over-burdened intellectual used to go around with an umbrella of the type and size used to protect patrons of seaside cafes from sun and shower. In times of shortage we shared a taxi, and he seemingly taking a liking to me, produced a large notebook and asked me my name. Deeming him to be rich and philanthropic I eagerly complied, and having recorded the details he put the book away. " Hmm," he mused, " there was a cricketer of that name who played for Lancashire." This slight geographical oversight may have had something to do with the fact that there was no happy sequel so far as I was concerned. During this time of shortage, a friend claims to have encountered two old-fashioned members enjoying their maiden trip on a bus. The elder acted as spokesman. " Young woman," he said to the baffled clippie. " Will ye drive us to 194 Malmsey Terrace."

Many and delightful are my memories of the past, and pleasant beyond words is my anticipation of the future regarding Lord's and all that it contains, sentiments which must go for every member worth his willow.

Far to the north lies Old Trafford, which last year celebrated its centenary. In 1856 the Manchester Cricket Club was ousted from its original ground, also at Old Trafford, to make room, improbably enough, for an Art Treasures Exhibition. It might have been some consolation to the departing cricketers had they been able to foresee the contrasting fates of Art and Sport. Whereas Old Trafford is one of the world's most famous cricket grounds, the Arts and Treasures Exhibition seems to have lapsed into obscurity.

From 1857 until 1864 the Manchester Cricket Club were

the sole occupants of the present ground. In 1864, however, the Lancashire County Cricket Club was formed, to
be closely identified with Old Trafford ever since. Twenty
years later the first Test Match was played at Old Trafford
and it is mildly surprising to reflect that, as an international ground, Manchester is senior to Lord's, if only
by a few days. It was perhaps an ill omen that there was
no play on the first day owing to rain.

If the surrounding district is hardly picturesque, the
ground itself is comely. Whatever the supposed shortcomings of the climate it is certainly conducive to the
growth of good grass and, in a country notable for the
quality of its turf, Old Trafford is pre-eminent. Both
playing area and practice ground are covered with a finely
woven carpet of such quality and colour as to carry any
architectural shortcomings. Not that there is much cause
for complaint on this score. The pavilion may not be
exactly a Taj Mahal (even allowing for the differences in
period, materials and purpose) but a thoughtful building
programme, especially in recent years, has given the
general scene a nice clean functional look. Such details
as a new rope pegged out by flags to mark the boundary
give a touch of gaiety and a pleasing effect of " finish."

But we are agreed, I hope, that where a place is an
active institution it is the people who run and frequent
it who chiefly determine its character and here, although
famous as an international ground, Old Trafford is essentially Lancastrian. While richly endowed with " atmosphere " there is above all a robust warmth which
permeates from Committee Room to free seats. On no
ground is the old player or, for that matter, the new one,
made more welcome.

The Lancashire public may have its grim moments, as
when their team is " oop agin it " with Yorkshire, but
there is always a basis of lusty good humour which comes
to the fore in times of crisis. When the traditions of Test
Match cricket tottered, and an exasperated and 22-stone
Armstrong staged a sit-down strike, sense of proportion

was restored by a genial suggestion that he could usefully
spend the time by rolling on the pitch. Years later a simi-
larly massive undergraduate, on missing a catch, heard
himself surrealistically described as "great big boomkin
with 'ands like maggots." It is no accident that so many
comedians come from Lancashire.

The men who made Old Trafford and those who continue to run it, and those who played and play on it, have
a rich tradition. To a modern generation the pioneers
are far-off ghosts, and at least two have been immortalised
as such ("Oh! my Hornby and my Barlow long ago").
There were the Rowleys, Royle, Steele and Briggs. Down
through the ages rings the exultant shout of fast-bowling
Crossland who cried out to the shattered clergyman:
"There goes your blankety pulpit." After him came Mold,
who committed the graver sin of bowling with bent elbow,
to be eventually discredited.

But the golden age of Old Trafford was later—an age
which owes much to Mr. Cardus for so vividly illuminating
it. It was dominated by the great MacLaren, graced by
Spooner and Tyldesley, and enlivened by Walter Brearley.

It is interesting to recall in these days of packed leg-
fields, the reaction of MacLaren to a modest formation of
short legs. Having surveyed them with withering contempt he inquired of the Australian captain what it meant
and, being dissatisfied with the answer, tersely ordered
their removal, a demand which was apparently complied
with.

Contemporaries say of Johnny Tyldesley that he was the
best sticky wicket player and the best square cutter the
game has ever seen. It must have been a particularly
satisfying combination of talents—not that there would
be much scope for the latter in modern times.

Midway between Lord's and Old Trafford lies Trent
Bridge, basking in a tradition as rich, in its way, as any
cricket ground in the world. Long years ago Old Clarke
laid out his pitch on the banks of the river, and charged
the spectators sixpence a head admission. A public,

hitherto accustomed to free entertainment in this line, delved into their pockets, but relieved their feelings by booing the enterprising promoter all the way to the wicket on his first appearance. By way of retaliation, he played upon them the age-old trick of pretending to be out when, in fact, he was not, and silencing their premature jubilation by an abrupt about turn.

It was from this headquarters that he organised and led his All England team which travelled an astonishing mileage, in view of the available transport. There is somewhere a dramatic account of one of their journeys through Cornwall in a coach, beset by the father and mother of all thunderstorms. The fulminations of the elements were well matched by the language of a fellow-passenger, a dashing soldier who had taken part in the charge at Balaclava. This was much to the distaste of the cricketers, who felt that, their last moment being near at hand, their reception elsewhere might well be adversely affected by their company. When George Parr sought help from a nearby cottage his nervous tension was in no way lessened to find himself peering down the bell mouth of a blunderbuss, and his explanations unavailing to a marksman who turned out to be deaf as an adder. All in all it hardly seemed to be the best preparation for a brisk hundred on the morrow.

The Nottinghamshire C.C.C. was founded in 1859 so is next senior to Surrey, as a continuing institution. In the eighties it dominated the championship as powerfully as Surrey and Yorkshire did at later dates. From its early beginnings it provided an abundant tributary to the broad river of cricket lore and character. George Parr's tree still stands to commemorate "The Lion of the North," although now obscured and overshadowed by a concrete stand. It probably flourished in splendid isolation when Shrewsbury led the professional batsmen of England. "Give me Arthur," said W.G. when asked who was (presumably) the second-best batsman of his time. I wonder if anyone ever hit the persevering Alfred Shaw over it?

Any such enterprise must have been fraught with hazard to judge from the tales of his meticulous accuracy.

The illustrious name of Gunn goes well back into Trent Bridge records, the towering William, followed by the stocky John and his brother George, the greatest virtuoso who ever took stance. "Young George" died tragically the other day in a car smash, but one hopes that some time again a Gunn will open the Notts innings.

In pre-war days I used to play for Sir Julien Cahn's team. John Gunn was umpire and Dick Burrows was scorer, and many a fine clack did we have together. John, going well in his 82nd year, has some wonderful reminiscences of the days of his uncle William, Hallam, A. O. Jones and many another hero. Perhaps my favourite of his old-time friends was "Topsy" Wass, who bowled fast leg-breaks and never had to shave. Amongst other adventures he had many a spirited contest with Charles Fry, verbal as well as athletic. When Charles stopped him in his run up, and asked that some boys by the screen might be shifted, the indignant Tom promised: "Next time tha' cooms 'ere we'll have pavilion shifted for thee." At that Charles said in a sinister tone: "You need shifting yourself, Wass" and proceeded to shift him to the tune of two hundred plus. Told by his captain to apologise to Sir Pelham Warner for his colourful comments on the run of play between them, he did so handsomely. As a shower drove the players from the field he galloped past with a contrite shout of "Bludy sorry for swearin', Sir."

In the twenties and early thirties Trent Bridge was a great joy to play on, for the wicket, although a beauty, was lightning fast and a satisfactory surface for the leg breaker. But visiting batsmen had to face "Lol" Larwood and Bill Voce, a wonderfully well matched pair of fast bowlers, so different in style but such a perfect balance. There must be few of them who can boast, as I can, of hitting Larwood with the new ball for a five. The story should really end there, but just in case anyone should blow the gaff, I am bound to say it wasn't quite as grand a gesture as it sounds. I don't know why they bothered to have a new ball because only Fred Price and myself were left, but anyway it hit the shoulder of my bat and went down to third man for two. The fielder, Joe Hardstaff, heaved it high over Ben Lilley's head and, there being no one in front of the wicket, we ran another three while short-leg chased it. I think with a little pressure we might have got another, which would have made the tale just that much better, but we were a bit jaded, and I had an idea that the next ball was going to be rather a good one. It was—just about as good as I have ever seen, and it ended the game there and then with a loud crash and a cloud of dust.

The wicket has grown progressively slower over the years and even such drastic action as digging it up and re-laying it seems to have had only a limited effect. It may be that new turf requires some time to settle down solidly on the subsoil.

Leeds is the one ground of the big five on which I have never played. Despite a number of visits to Yorkshire I have only played at Bradford, where Middlesex always went in the thirties. Until the last series it had not been a very lucky ground for England against Australia, and in my playing time was chiefly remarkable for Bradman's tremendous onslaughts of 1930 and 1934. I was fortunate in not taking part in either, for they happened on a couple of rare good wickets. The English leg-breaker was Dick Tyldesley, who got little work on the ball, but a packet on his poor old legs at mid-on. After an unending series of steady but fruitless pursuits to the boundary, he heaved his eighteen stone into a chair and announced that, as far as Test Matches were concerned, all he wanted was to get back to Manchester and get his " poomps " on.

The triumphant batsman, fresh as a daisy, at 300-odd not out, casually referred to his efforts as " a nice bit of practice for to-morrow."

I did, however, play at the Oval, where Don was rather less successful, only scoring 232, but it is fair to say there was some doubt about his dismissal, for some thought he hadn't touched the ball when given out caught behind. It was on a very special Oval wicket specially prepared for a Test Match and a discouraging outlook for any bowler. In the ordinary way the Oval, like Trent Bridge, was not so very unkind to my type of bowler, for it also had a certain degree of pace. The Surrey batting order, on the other hand, used to be a fair day's work for any attack when it started with Hobbs, Sandham, Shepherd, Ducat, Jardine, Holmes, Fender. The bowling was rather less impressive and, perforce, relied largely on endurance. Having made a handsome total, Surrey's hopes of getting the opposition out depended chiefly on Fender, Peach, patience and providence.

The tale is told of one old stalwart who, grown wise in his generation, may be called Wiseman. When he awoke to sunny summer's morn and the thought of another day in the field was altogether too much for him, he would step round to the local post office and despatch a telegram which read: " Wiseman ill. Signed Wiseman " before returning to lend his side spiritual support from his favourite armchair.

Although these five have been the chosen grounds for major Test Matches during the present century, Edgbaston has strong claims for inclusion, which, indeed, have now been recognised. Birmingham is a vast city and, with much alteration and addition to the amenities and accommodation, has now got a magnificent ground. The last Test Match played there against the West Indies must rank as one of the more dramatic played anywhere.

No doubt the great urban grounds are the bastions of County cricket. It is at Lord's, Trent Bridge, Leeds and Old Trafford that giants, if not actually bred, are matured, Test Matches are played and cricket history made. But it is with joy in his heart that the inhabitant of one of these strongholds packs his bag after a spell of home matches, and sets out for the freer, fresher atmosphere of a more rustic neighbour's ground.

Of course many committees would like to use the many first class club grounds within their boundaries in addition to the civic centre, so to speak, but this is seldom economically possible. Essex, on the other hand, many years ago went the whole hog and, having sold their town ground, started playing all round the county. It was a decision that few have regretted.

Did you ever play cricket at Leyton in days gone by? It was not, I fear, a very exhilarating experience. If the player lived or stayed in London he started the morning by setting forth from the gloom of Liverpool Street station, or went skidding along the endless miles of tram rails, which wound through some of the less attractive of London's thoroughfares. On arrival his welcome would be warm and friendly, and he would know that the flawless turf before him had cradled many great and seen much great play. But all this, even with a hundred or seven wickets tossed in, could never quite outweigh the general depression of the surroundings. If it rained, woe unto all.

I know that in its hey-day Leyton boasted Perrin, McGahey, Reeves, Douglas and Gillingham, a cricketing Pickwick Papers in themselves, but that is another story. What I want to say at the moment is how different is the lot of the cricketer playing in Essex now.

Either he bounds about in the ozone of a seaside resort, or he breathes the pure air of some market town nestling in the midst of pleasant farming country. At Colchester, if he is historically minded, his thoughts may occasionally wander towards the wealth of lore and legend about him. The crowd, not being surfeited with first class cricket, is friendly and responsive, and as like as not he stays in an old inn as picturesquely Dickensian as the company mentioned above.

Kent, as befitting "The Garden of England," has probably got the largest selection of cricket grounds where rural beauty blends with suitability for county cricket. Canterbury is usually accepted as the queen, but they are all pretty good. I have a personal bias for Dover, with its natural green grandstand at the pavilion end, but possibly this is not entirely a taste for natural beauty. It may be because, over twenty years ago, I delivered seventeen rather indifferent overs in a fourth innings there and got seven wickets. One of these was Frank Woolley, caught at the wicket off a full toss. This affected the company with the same awful delight as if, in earlier years, they had seen the headmaster go for six on a banana peel. I remember the same day fielding mid-off, deep mid-off and finally very long-off to three successive balls, which Charlie Wright hit high over my head into a wood far behind my last position.

Our itinerary used to take us from Kent across London to Paddington and the West Country, to which my personal fancy has always inclined. The G.W.R. (sorry, Western Region) even now so different that it might be operating on the seven-foot gauge, leads to many a fair cricket ground.

To the Parks at Oxford, set in the tranquil beauty of its surrounding trees, a beauty undisturbed by clanging tram or beery barracker, but enhanced by the mellow sounds of a summer's day in the country and the chime of ancient bells. Moreover, the wicket, though inclined to slowness, always gives promise of a little turn. And what grandeur is lent to the pavilion by the presence of these gigantic intellects, so obviously oscillating between the first wicket and the fourth dimension.

And so, as the film says, we take a long farewell of Oxford and an easy journey to Worcester, another ground of uncommon beauty or at least of uncommonly beautiful aspects. Its vivid green is largely due to the fact that practically every winter, when the Severn rises, the ground is submerged under several feet of water. One member used annually to swim across the ground, while another gaffed a sizable salmon from the rails of the pavilion.

It is due to this inundation that the pavilion is built up on timber piles, whereby hangs another tale. Changing there one morning on the second day of the match, Arthur Dolphin, the Yorkshire keeper, followed his life-long habit of arraying himself fully for the field then stepping into his boots, where they stood overnight, and lacing them up. On this occasion he was unaware that his team mate, George Macaulay, had driven a couple of six-inch nails through the soles and, taking advantage of the structure, bent them back under the floor. When the glad cry "All aboard" went up, poor old "Dolly" must have feared a sudden bout of locomotor ataxia.

On again further west to Taunton, a gracious ground on which cricket has always been graciously played. The vivid memory of being driven into the far distant river by Guy Earle cannot lessen my affection for it. In a nostalgic moment the other day I turned up the map of Taunton ground in Wisden, and was intrigued by a feature prominently marked "flower pot." It must indeed be a remarkable member of its species to be thus commemorated. Would it be "the Biggest Aspidistra in the World" of which Miss Fields used to sing? Did the groundsman carry off a prize at Chelsea, or had the pot, or spot, some romantic association for the cartographer? Next time in Taunton I'll try and find out.

Well, I seem to have pottered and dallied so much on the way that there is little time to say anything of the County grounds of neighbouring Gloucester with all their undoubted attractions, where one is ever aware of the benign influence of "W.G.," to say nothing of the beady eye of Uncle Pocock.

Nor to dwell on the character of Hove, with the tang of ozone and the slight sea mist, beloved of the new ball bowler.

But then there are tens of thousands of cricket grounds within the lands of Batter's Castle. Be they grand as Lord's, or beautiful as Cape Town, or merely a strip of waste land beside the local gas-works, they have a magic and a promise for some cricketer.

Be he old or young, may he prosper—and be grateful.

THE PAVILION LIBRARY

All books from the Pavilion Cricket Library are available through your local bookshop or can be ordered direct from Pavilion Books Ltd.

	hardback	paperback
Through the Caribbean Alan Ross	£10.95	£5.95
Hirst and Rhodes A. A. Thomson	£10.95	£5.95
Two Summers at the Tests John Arlott	£10.95	£5.95
Batter's Castle Ian Peebles	£10.95	£5.95
The Ashes Crown the Year Jack Fingleton	£10.95	£5.95
Life Worth Living C. B. Fry	£10.95	£5.95
Cricket Crisis Jack Fingleton	£9.95	£4.95
Brightly Fades the Don Jack Fingleton	£9.95	£4.95
Cricket Country Edmund Blunden	£9.95	£4.95
Odd Men In A. A. Thomson	£9.95	£4.95
Crusoe on Cricket R. C. Robertson-Glasgow	£9.95	£4.95
Benny Green's **Cricket Archive**	£9.95	£4.95

Write to Pavilion Books Ltd.
    196 Shaftesbury Avenue
    London WC2H 8JL

Please enclose cheque or postal order for the cover price plus postage

UK   55p for first book
        24p for each additional book to a maximum of £1.75

Overseas   £1.05 for first book
                    35p for each additional book to a maximum of £2.80

Pavilion Books reserve the right to show new retail prices on covers which may differ from those previously advertised in the text or elsewhere and to increase postal rates in accordance with the Post Office.